SMURF IN WANDERLAND
DAVID WILLIAMS

CURRENCY PRESS

RIVERSIDE | NATIONAL THEATRE OF PARRAMATTA

GRIFFIN THEATRE COMPANY

CURRENCY PLAYS

First published in 2017
by Currency Press Pty Ltd,
PO Box 2287, Strawberry Hills, NSW, 2012, Australia
enquiries@currency.com.au
www.currency.com.au

in association with National Theatre of Parramatta and Griffin Theatre Company

Cataloguing-in-publication data for this title is available from the National
Library of Australia website: www.nla.gov.au

Typeset by Dean Nottle for Currency Press.
National Theatre of Parramatta cover:

  Design by Tristan Ceddia
  Photography by Eric Berry.
Griffin Theatre Company cover:
  Design by RE:
  Photography by Brett Boardman.
Both covers show David Williams.

Contents

Currency Press acknowledges the Traditional Owners of the Country on which we live and work. We pay our respects to all Aboriginal and Torres Strait Islander Elders, past and present.

Smurf in Wanderland was first produced by National Theatre of Parramatta and Griffin Theatre Company at the Riverside Theatres, Parramatta, on 20 April 2017, with the following crew:

Performer, David Williams
Director, Lee Lewis
Set and Costume Designer, Charles Davis
Lighting Designer, Luiz Pampolha
Sound Designer and Composer, James Brown
Dramaturg, Kate Worsley
Creative Futures Participant, Nick Atkins
Stage Manager, Kirsty Walker
Production Manager, Damion Holling

CHARACTER

DAVID, a Sydney FC supporter

SETTING

Various locations across Sydney, with regular returns to Pirtek Stadium, Parramatta.

This play went to press before the end of rehearsals and may differ from the play as performed.

ACT ONE

INTRO

Good evening, everyone, and welcome to *Smurf in Wanderland*.

My name is David Williams, and I'll be your host tonight.

Just before kick-off, a few small notes, a bit of housekeeping, some clarifications.

Firstly, for those who might not be aware, this is a show about *football* and *Sydney*.

And just to be clear, when I say football, I mean the game with the round ball that you play with your feet, sometimes referred to as 'soccer'.

Okay?

So, if anyone is concerned about their safety, I'll just point out that the nearest emergency exits are here and here.

> *He points.*

Okay, great.

So if everyone is feeling safe, some important information for context.

So, this show is concerned with two football teams, Sydney FC and the Western Sydney Wanderers.

For those of you who aren't aware, a 'Smurf' is a nickname for a Sydney FC supporter.

It's about the sky-blue colours.

By contrast, the Wanderers' colours are red and black.

Just in case anyone here didn't know that.

And 'Wanderland' is what Pirtek Stadium is re-branded during Western Sydney Wanderers' home games.

I hope that goes some of the way to explain the title of tonight's performance.

Some parts of the show will reference things that happen in football games, and there'll be the occasional moment of good-natured audience inclusion.

If anyone is truly terrified by this, a reminder that the nearest
emergency exits are here and here.

He points.

Given the show *is* about two teams, I have taken the liberty of dividing
the audience in half.

Given that this is the slightly more easterly side of the theatre, I've
cast [*indicating*] this half of the audience as Sydney FC fans.

And given that this side of the theatre has a slightly more westerly
aspect, tonight you will be Western Sydney Wanderers fans.

If anyone feels that they are now sitting in the wrong place, now is
your chance to move.

Really.

You really can change sides now if you want. But this is your *only*
chance.

Don't worry—it's not permanent.

If you've found yourself stuck in the 'wrong' supporter side, please
just take tonight's performance as an opportunity to role-play.

To walk in the shoes of the other half of the city for an hour and a half.

Okay?

Great.

And a reminder to anyone who is feeling threatened by all of this talk
about soccer and choice and inclusion and Smurfs and participation,
a reminder that the nearest emergency exits are here and here.

He points.

Great! So, is everyone sitting in the correct place?

Nice one.

At various times, this show will be punctuated by chants and songs
sung by supporters of each team.

Please join in.

So, tonight's show will be about ninety minutes long, in two forty-five
minute halves.

Plus stoppage time added on.

This show is going to jump around in time quite a lot, from the 1960s to the present day. But much of the show will focus on Season Nine of the A-League, from October 2013 to May 2014.

Season Nine was important for a few reasons—it was the second year of the unexpectedly wild rise of the new team on the block, the Western Sydney Wanderers, and it was the final season played by marquee players Alessandro Del Piero (for Sydney FC) and Shinji Ono (for Western Sydney Wanderers).

It also marked the final season for foundation Sydney FC player Terry McFlynn, who retired after a decade with the club, the last man left standing from Season One back in 2005/2006.

Terry's not really in this show as much as he should be, but he's an important player for the club.

This is the program for his farewell game.

He points to a match program on the wall.

Season Nine saw fan revolts (from Sydney FC members, who demanded the sacking of coach Frank Farina) and threats of points being deducted from the Western Sydney Wanderers for alleged fan misbehaviour after a match in Melbourne.

It's fair to say that Season Nine was not a great one for Sydney FC, and so it feels strange to be performing this show right now, in 2017, at the end of Sydney's most successful season in a long time.

It's still not quite real to me that we've been top of the league all season long.[1]

I kept thinking that reality would reassert itself and Sydney would fall apart. Again.

And there have indeed been stumbles that made that seem likely.

But the team has got on with it and done the business.

Exciting.

But still not quite real.

But anyway, this show focuses on being a fan in all of the *other* years.

The not-so-golden years.

---

[1] This script went to press after Sydney FC's 1–0 win over Melbourne Victory, leaving them 11 points ahead of second place. So whilst it is mathematically possible that Sydney will not win the league, this is unlikely.

The years when you have to think long and hard about whether the frustration is worth it.

The years when you hate it, but you are compelled to keep going back to games.

Just in case your team magically gets better.

Because they might.

They just might.

And so perhaps some elements of tonight's show might be instructive to Wanderers fans.

There are lots of things that are *not* in tonight's show.

I'm not going to talk about this years' bewildering mid-season goalkeeper exchange.

I'm not going to talk about snakes.

I'm not going to talk about banners with giant penises.

I'm not going to talk about the redevelopment of Parramatta Stadium and the temporary shift to Spotless Stadium.

Which is probably for the best.

And Tim Cahill is not in my story.

Anywhere.

Okay, so the players are on the pitch, and the referee checks his watch. Here we go.

KICK OFF!

> *A whistle blows and the game clock begins.*

GAME 1—PRELUDE

So, it's twentieth October 2013.

Round Two of Season Nine.

Western Sydney Wanderers versus Wellington Phoenix.

The first Wanderers home game of the 2013/2014 season.

It's a sunny Sunday afternoon, and I'm heading to Wanderland, the unofficial name for Pirtek Stadium in Parramatta.

> *He removes his jacket to reveal a sky-blue jersey underneath.*

I'm wearing my sky blue, relatively new Del Piero number ten Sydney FC jersey.

And my red Wanderers member lanyard.

I get on the train at Sydenham, and change trains at Redfern.

As the train continues westward, more and more people in red and black jerseys start to fill the seats. When I get off the train at Parramatta station, there is a veritable sea of red and black shuffling towards the exits.

One guy turns around to look at me as I stand behind him on the escalator.

'Where's Western Sydney?' he says. 'Where is it?'

'It's all around us,' I answer.

'Then why are *you here*?'

He's not angry. Or threatening.

But his question is emphatic.

'Why are *you here*?'

It's a good question.

Why am I heading over to a Western Sydney Wanderers game?

Why am I wearing the colours of their local rival, Sydney FC?

The second question is easy—Sydney FC is my team, and I've been a member for almost a decade.

For my sins.

The first question is more complicated.

Why am I *here*?

WHY AM I HERE?

I'm going to jump back in time a bit.

A bit over fifty years.

My mother's family emigrated from Liverpool, England, arriving in Sydney by ocean liner in November 1963.

Upon landing in Sydney, her father, my grandfather, was offered the choice of two houses for the newly arrived family—a big house on a long block attached to the water in Haberfield, or a newly built house in a new suburb called Greystanes.

In Liverpool, England, only very poor people lived near the water—it was filthy, dirty, undesirable.

No-one in their right mind would possibly *choose* to live next to the water.

So my grandfather chose to settle the family in Greystanes, even though he had no idea how far out it was.

For those of you don't know, Greystanes is two suburbs south-west of Parramatta, about equidistant between Parramatta and Blacktown.

My father grew up in the neighbouring suburb of South Wentworthville, the eldest of five boys.

My parents met at church, at St Matthew's, in nearby Merrylands West, and married in 1974.

Obviously I'm summarising a lot here.

My parents were not football fans at all, and so had the very poor judgment of getting married on FA Cup final night.

Liverpool were playing, and so a large number of my mother's relatives, a number of whom had come over from overseas[2], insisted that the reception be furnished with a television so that they could all watch the game in the corner.

For what it's worth, when I asked my father about this last year, he had absolutely no memory of it.

He told me that he had no idea that they were watching a football game that night.

So he was oblivious to Liverpool defeating Newcastle United three-nil that night to win only their second FA Cup, their first in ten years. Their only previous victory was in 1965.

Presumably the expat Liverpudlians at my parents' wedding had a good time that evening.

In August 1975, I was born at the now-closed Parramatta District Hospital, the site of which incidentally was across the river from where Pirtek Stadium, aka Wanderland, stands today.

At the time, my parents lived in Merrylands, one suburb south of Parramatta, but I have no memory of that house.

We moved to Bradman Street, Greystanes, in 1976, with my parents paying forty-nine thousand dollars for the house. A bit more than

---

[2]   I know that this implies England, but these relatives, whilst also migrants from Liverpool, actually came across from New Zealand for the wedding.

they could really afford at the time, but my dad *really* liked the fact it had a pool.

He's still very proud of that pool.

The Greystanes that I remember had lots of empty blocks with horses on them.

Suburbia ended at Greystanes Road.

It was the decade in which the Parramatta Eels dominated the rugby league. But rugby league was never my thing.

The primary school was across the road.

Public transport was … well, there wasn't much of it, just the occasional bus.

In the West of my childhood, you drove everywhere.

I went to primary school in Greystanes, then high school in Glenfield.

Glenfield is quite a way south, past Liverpool on the way to Campbelltown.

I had to get the bus from Greystanes to Merrylands, then a train from Merrylands to Glenfield. Over an hour's travel each way.

Basically, if I missed the seven-twelve a.m. bus, I was late to school, unless Dad drove me to the train station on his way to work in Auburn.

Auburn, by the way, is two suburbs south-east of Parramatta.

I was late to school … regularly.

To be completely honest, this wasn't always by accident.

Especially when there was Maths in the first period of the day.

The parents of one of my high school friends ran a restaurant in Cabramatta, which is about three-quarters of the way from Merrylands to Glenfield.

And every now and then we could exploit the fact that they didn't speak much English by turning up at the restaurant in the late morning.

Because obviously, if there were a *group* of us, then there must be a legitimate *reason* for us not to be in school.

I was never quite sure how my friend Chi justified this to his parents, but it seemed to work.

So yes, there were some advantages to long commutes across the south-western suburbs to school.

Afterwards, I studied theatre at the University of Western Sydney, Nepean, in Kingswood, near Penrith. Which is quite a way west, near the foot of the Blue Mountains.

My first job was at Kmart Fairfield West, two suburbs south-west of Greystanes.

I started on the check-outs, and then took over the loading dock after the manager there had a serious back injury. After that, store was closed down, I was transferred to Kmart Merrylands and worked the loading dock there.

Whilst at university I joined an indoor football team organised by some of the guys from my church choir (yes, I was in a church choir for several years, at St John's Parramatta; you, know, the big church on Church Street in Parramatta).

Our football team was called the Parramatta Pirates.

Yes, a terrible name.

And we had a terrible uniform to go with it—pale blue with yellow trim. Super ugly.

After the first year we switched uniforms, and played in Bayern Munich jerseys—red and blue vertical stripes with a white collar.

No-one had any particular attachment to Bayern Munich, it was just that the shop had them on sale.

We played at an indoor sports centre out in Bonnyrigg.

Now Bonnyrigg is …

Actually, it doesn't really matter where Bonnyrigg is.

We were a terrible team.

We would lose every game twenty–nil.

Sometimes twenty-one–one.

Which was exciting.

We scored a goal!

We were obviously in the lowest league, but there were other competitions played in the same sports centre. The later comp was filled with passionate and skilful players. It was really fun to watch, and everyone, including the spectators, took it very seriously. Every few weeks there would be an on-field bust-up, and at least once that I remember, spectators leapt onto the field to get in on the action.

I finally moved out of home in Greystanes in 1996 when I landed my first professional theatre job—three months performing with the now-defunct, but much celebrated Sidetrack Performance Group.

Sidetrack was based in Marrickville, which is about twenty-one and a half kilometres east-south-east of Parramatta. So, that puts it in the so-called 'Inner West' of Sydney.

There really weren't any theatre jobs in western Sydney, not in the mid-nineties anyway.

There were new venues starting to open—like Riverside Theatres Parramatta—so there were opportunities for people to get onstage for fun. I'd done that—starting with joining the Cumberland *Gang Show* in 1985.

In case anyone is unfamiliar with the *Gang Show*, it's a Scouts and Guides musical variety show. If you can imagine that.

The *Gang Show* was one of the first shows to perform at the new Riverside Theatres Parramatta when it opened in 1988, and I was there with them on that stage, at age twelve. It's still running today, and performs in the July school holidays.

If you're interested.

So you could get on the stage for fun or for the love of it. But if you wanted to make a living out of theatre, then staying in the West was not an option.

So I took the job in Marrickville.

To get there from Greystanes I had to make sure I was on the M4 as close to six a.m. as possible, so as to get to rehearsals on time.

This was in the days when the M4 toll was still payable—two dollars and seventy-five cents each way.

Anyway, this commute got really boring really quickly, and so I finally moved into a share house in Balmain, which is about twenty-one kilometres east of Parramatta.

So quite a lot closer to my new job in Marrickville.

Twenty years later, Marrickville is where I now call home.

I mention all of this to indicate that the first twenty-plus years of my
    life involved crisscrossing Greater Western Sydney. Which was
    intrinsically embedded within, and connected to, the rest of Sydney.

And this fact was unremarkable.

Everyone did it.

Everyone still does it.

And yet, twenty-plus years later, the idea of some psycho-geographic
    divide between the 'West' and everywhere else in Sydney is talked
    about as if it is an uncontested and uncontestable fact.

But in October 2013, when asked by the guy on the escalator in
    Parramatta station:

'Why are you here?' I don't mention any of this.

I simply smile and say:

'I like football.'

> *A pause.*

GAME 1, CONTINUED

A couple of nights previously, I had told my parents that I would be
    going to the Wanderers game today wearing my Sydney FC jersey.

My mother was horrified.

She had in mind perhaps a childhood memory of the streets of
    Liverpool, England, where blue Everton shirts received a hostile
    reception in the 'wrong' part of town.

But I remained confident that the Parramatta that I had grown up in
    wasn't like that.

Pretty confident.

Well, quietly confident.

I exit the station at Parramatta and join the crowds heading to the
    stadium.

Most people don't notice me, or at least choose to ignore me.

One guy walking past says, 'Sydney FC, really?'

'Really,' I reply in a friendly tone.

'You guys played last night. You got caned.'

'Yeah. We played terribly.'

He doesn't really know what to say after that, and so we just keep walking along.

As we continue down Church Street there are lots of shouts from the distance:

'FOUR-NIL!'

'FOUR-NIL!'

Which was fair enough—Sydney FC *did* lose four-nil in Brisbane the previous night.

But it's early in the season, so there's still hope for improvement.

So I have hope.

I've arranged to walk part of the way to the stadium with Walter, a work colleague and Wanderers fan, and his brother Louis.

I haven't met Louis before.

We rendezvous part-way down Church Street, and shortly after we meet up, Louis wants to stop and grab something to eat at Oporto.

I think he'd come straight from work, and he wasn't a big fan of the food options at the stadium.

Something like that.

Anyway, we step inside, and the sea of red and black continues to flow past outside.

From inside Oporto, Louis spies someone walking past in a Liverpool jersey.

'Ah, a Liverpool shirt,' he says.

'I'll get him later. I dunno why, but I always hate them.'

I'm not sure what's with the Liverpool-hating, but I'm careful not to mention my (loose) family connection to that team.

After all, I've just met this guy.

Actually, while we're walking I see quite a few English Premier League team jerseys—Manchester United, Manchester City, more Liverpool jerseys. There's also a smattering of Barcelona, Brazil and even a Bayern Munich jersey.

But mostly the red and black of Western Sydney Wanderers.

And me, in sky blue.

Arriving at Pirtek Stadium, I join the pre-game queue to pick up my Wanderers member's pack.

Standing in the queue with hundreds of other Wanderers members whilst wearing my Sydney FC jersey, I get some baffled looks.

The woman at the counter looks up my name and ticks me off the list, handing me my pack.

> *He holds up his member's pack, unzips it, and pulls a range of merchandise from inside it.*

A small cooler bag.

A fridge magnet with a fixtures list on it.

A cap.

A keyring.

And a bumper sticker.

'You know,' says the woman helpfully, 'The merchandise caravan is just over there. You can get the right shirt.'

I politely suggest to her that it's probably too soon for that.

'Ah!' she says.

'We'll convert you yet! You'll be my third. The last ones I converted were from Newcastle. And they live up there!'

I smile and thank her.

I smile a lot.

Walking around to my entrance gate, there's a guy behind the stadium fence holding a beer.

He sees me, laughs, points and chants:

'WHO ARE YA? WHO ARE YA? WHO ARE YA?'

We share a smile.

More smiling.

I walk into the gate.

After scanning my ticket the security guard points at my sky-blue shirt and says:

'You got something to cover that, mate?'

I smile.

I go to my seat.

Bay forty-three, Row N, seat seventy-nine.

It's on the end of a row.

Which could be convenient.

We'll see.

I smile at my new neighbours, a couple with two small kids, all kitted out in Wanderers gear.

They smile back.

The game is really good, with the teams more closely matched than I thought they'd be.

The view from my seat is great, and the vibe at the stadium is lively.

The RBB—that's the Red and Black Bloc, the active supporter group for the Wanderers—are lots of fun to watch, energetically cheering the whole match long.

The chants ring around the stadium.

Actually, we could have a go at this chant.

[*Indicating*] This one's for you, my friends in the western side of the audience.

Okay, it's a pretty simple call-and-response chant.

I say, 'Who do we sing for?'

And you, as the Wanderers fans, you say, 'We sing for Wanderers!'

It's pretty easy. Ready?

[*Calling*] WHO DO WE SING FOR?

> *The Western audience responds: WE SING FOR WANDERERS!*

WHO DO WE SING FOR?

> *Western audience response: WE SING FOR WANDERERS!*

We'll do one more.

WHO DO WE SING FOR?

> *Western audience response: WE SING FOR WANDERERS!*

Thanks, guys, that's fantastic.

The energy at the stadium is great.

I enjoy the spectacle.

At the final whistle it's a one-all draw.

Western Sydney should have had it wrapped up, but they just lost a bit of concentration I think, and Wellington's coach Ernie Merrick had done his homework well.

Wanderers coach Tony Popovic did not seem happy at any point during the game.

Later, I discovered that he always looks like this.

Game over, I exit the stadium and join the crowds walking back to the train station.

Whilst walking in a big crowd of Western Sydney supporters, I get numerous call-outs from strangers.

'Faggot.'

'Nice shirt, ya dickhead.'

And my favourite:

'Where'd ya get your shirt? Gay cunts R us?'

I smile more.

Crossing Prince Alfred Park, a guy in front of me drops a ten-dollar note and keeps walking, oblivious.

I chase him down, tap him on the shoulder and give it back to him.

He looks me up and down.

'Not bad for a Smurf,' he says.

He commiserates the four-nil drubbing from the previous night, and we look forward to next week's match, where Sydney FC will play Western Sydney Wanderers at Moore Park.

The first 'Sydney derby' for the season.

We keep walking.

Back at Parramatta train station, on the escalator up to the platform, a man in a Wanderers jersey points to the Sydney FC logo on my shirt and says:

'So you admit, it's *East* Sydney. Not *Sydney*. You admit that?'

'That's where I'm going,' I say. 'I'm heading back east.'

Changing trains again at Redfern, another Wanderers fan ahead of me on the escalator down to Platform Twelve turns around, and does a double take.

'Hey, mate, what happened in Brisbane last night?'

I can only confess, 'I don't know. I think we left our team back in
   Sydney.'

We have a polite conversation whilst awaiting the next train, agreeing
   that the Wanderers really should have won tonight, that they had a
   bit of bad luck, and the midfield didn't really connect.

I agreed, adding that they really missed Aaron Mooy, subbed off
   injured in the tenth minute after a hard tackle.

He says it shouldn't matter.

'We've got so much quality.'

FIRST DERBY

Okay. Jumping forward one week.

Saturday October twenty-six, 2013.

Sydney FC versus Western Sydney Wanderers.

The first Sydney derby for Season Nine.

Just in case there's anyone who is not a sports fan here tonight, who
   has no idea what a 'derby' is, derbies are generally games played
   between local, or geographically close teams.

So the rivalries are more intense, the stakes seem higher, and, well,
   there's just more people in the crowd.

Everyone has more to prove in a derby.

Everyone brags more about a derby win.

And derby losses feel more devastating.

Sometimes, it doesn't seem to really matter how the rest of season is
   going, so long as we can beat the other Sydney team.

The banter between fans and players steps up a notch.

The *tifo*—that's the special match displays of signs and flags and
   choreographed movement routines by the active supporters—are
   always of a higher class for derbies.

The passionate fans are, well, more passionate.

And much, much louder.

Derby games are fantastic.

The best thing about derbies is the atmosphere.

Big crowds and high stakes equals lots of noise.

Let's build a bit of atmosphere here.

So, another call-and-response chant, this time from our Sydney FC fans here.

Really, really simple, this one.

Okay, so in this chant, we just repeat the same things each time.

The Cove—that's the Sydney FC active support group, who stand at the northern end of the stadium at Moore Park—they start.

I'm not a Cove member, but tonight I'm going to channel them.

Okay, so I say, 'Sydney', and then you say, 'Sydney'.

And then you just repeat everything else that I say.

Easy.

Let's try it.

SYDNEY!

>   *Sydney FC audience response: SYDNEY!*

C'MON, YOU BOYS IN BLUE!

>   *Sydney FC audience response: C'MON, YOU BOYS IN BLUE!*

SYDNEY IS SKY BLUE!

>   *Sydney FC audience response: SYDNEY IS SKY BLUE!*

Okay, that's great.

But *atmosphere*, that needs something else.

Let's step it up.

Alright, are we ready?

Both sides, both call-and-response chants.

Remember how they went?

I'll lead both.

SYDNEY!

>   *Sydney FC audience response: SYDNEY!*

WHO DO WE SING FOR?!

>   *Western audience response: WE SING FOR WANDERERS!*

SYDNEY!

>   *Sydney FC audience response: SYDNEY!*

WHO DO WE SING FOR?!

> *Western audience response: WE SING FOR WANDERERS!*

C'MON YOU BOYS IN BLUE!

> *Sydney FC audience response: C'MON, YOU BOYS IN BLUE!*

WHO DO WE SING FOR?!

> *Western audience response: WE SING FOR WANDERERS!*

SYDNEY IS SKY BLUE!

> *Sydney FC audience response: SYDNEY IS SKY BLUE!*

WHO DO WE SING FOR?!

> *Western audience response: WE SING FOR WANDERERS!*

Fantastic. Now you're getting it.

Allianz Stadium in Moore Park is sold out, so that's a crowd of over forty thousand fans. It's super loud as the two sets of fans try and outdo each other.

The game starts.

And if you're a Sydney FC fan like me, it's not pretty.

The opening goal was in the eleventh minute, from Western Sydney's Iacopo La Rocca.

The second goal, in the twenty-sixth minute, featured some magic from Western Sydney's Shinji Ono, who almost danced in the goal mouth with an unbelievable strike.

It was pretty incredible.

Ono does a little flick that loops the ball over the heads of two defenders.

He keeps running toward goal.

The ball falls behind him, but he sees it, spins, dives, sticks his leg out and pokes the ball into the bottom corner of the net with his right foot.

Sydney FC goalkeeper Vedran Janjetovic barely had time to react.

The red and black half of the crowd goes crazy.

Join in if you know it, Wanderers fans! The tune is the nineties pop song 'No Limits'.

He chants:

> ONO
> ONO, ONO
> ONO, ONO
> ONO
> SHINJI ONO!
>
> ONO
> ONO, ONO
> ONO, ONO
> ONO
> SHINJI ONO!
>
> ONO
> ONO, ONO
> ONO, ONO
> ONO
> SHINJI ONO![3]

A flurry of fouls and yellow cards in the second half saw out the match.

We never looked like coming back.

After the four-nil loss to Brisbane the previous weekend and now this second loss, it was looking like it was going to be yet another long, hard season.

But this was *not* how the story was supposed to unfold.

Because one year earlier, everything had changed.

One year earlier, Alessandro Del Piero arrived in Sydney.

And a fairytale was supposed to begin.

DEL PIERO

I'm going to jump back in time a little over one year from that derby game.

Back to September 2012.

---

[3] Perhaps unsurprisingly, this same tune is now used in 2016/17 for goal celebration chants when Sydney FC's new striker, nicknamed 'Bobo', scores.

Sydney FC dropped the bombshell that they had signed legendary Italian striker Alessandro Del Piero on a deal rumoured to be more than two million dollars per year.

Del Piero had spent nineteen seasons at Juventus, one of the biggest Italian clubs. He'd won league titles, European titles, even a World Cup. Basically he'd won everything there is to win in football.

He was a big, big name.

It was simply unbelievable that Del Piero would come and play for Sydney.

It was momentous news.

No-one had seen it coming.

Sydney FC had pulled out all the stops to lure Del Piero to Australia, including a letter from then- Prime Minister Julia Gillard.

'Football in Australia continues to go from strength to strength,' she wrote.

'And I know Mr Del Piero would inspire an entire generation of young Australians to get involved in the game at a critical time in its growth.'[4]

It worked.

Much to the excited surprise of the world's sports media, Del Piero signed.

Sydney FC fans, and even the other A-League teams, were thrilled.

This is Sydney FC Chairman Scott Barlow:

'This is huge for Sydney FC, huge for the A-League and huge for Australian football. We feel honoured that Alessandro has decided to play for Sydney FC and we share his excitement that a move to Sydney FC will create a lasting legacy for football in this country.'[5]

The great man himself?

---

[4] 'Letter from Australian Prime Minister Julia Gillard helped get Alessandro Del Piero deal over the line'. news.com.au, September 8, 2012.

[5] Sebastian Hassett, 'The $2 Million Man', *Sydney Morning Herald,* September 1, 2012.

Well, upon arrival at Sydney airport to rapturous applause, Del Piero said to the waiting TV cameras:

'I am not here for the end of my career, but for the start of my new career. I want to win some. I play to win.'[6]

His first home game at Allianz Stadium was against Newcastle Jets, and it was a huge event, attended by more than thirty-five thousand people.

From my vantage point it seemed that pretty much every Italian in Sydney was at the stadium on that day.

I was surrounded by families excitedly chattering away whilst wearing a mix of royal blue Italian national team, and black and white Juventus jerseys.

It seemed that thousands of people had already bought the newly issued Del Piero Sydney FC jerseys, like the one that I'm wearing. At one hundred and ten dollars per shirt, that must have been millions of dollars into Sydney FC's coffers.

(I must confess that my Del Piero jersey was purchased much later, in an end-of-season sale. It was reduced to seventy-five dollars. It was still very far from cheap. But I justified it as an early birthday present.)

Every time Del Piero touched the ball, the people around me stood up and started filming with their iPads.

Everyone seemed to have iPads …

They didn't seem to really care much about the game, only the maestro on the ball.

The buzz around the stadium was electric.

Sydney lost this game as well, three-two.

But Del Piero delivered the moment of magic that we had all been waiting for—a glorious free kick in the twenty-sixth minute.

Del Piero was fouled right in line with where I was sitting, and awarded a free kick.

From about twenty-five metres out, and at a challenging angle, Del Piero curved the ball over the wall of Newcastle players and into the back of the net.

---

[6] Joe Gorman, 'The Del Piero Effect', *Leopold Method 1*, 2014, page 23.

It looked impossible and effortless.

It was unbelievable.

Like everyone else, I was on my feet, shouting with incomprehensible joy.

Sydney fans, join in if you know it.

He chants.

> ALE, ALE,
> ALE, ALE, ALE,
> ALESSANDRO DEL PIERO,
> HE IS SYDNEY'S NUMBER TEN!
>
> ALE, ALE,
> ALE, ALE, ALE,
> ALESSANDRO DEL PIERO,
> HE IS SYDNEY'S NUMBER TEN!

It didn't seem to matter that we'd lost the game.

We had seen a glimpse of greatness, and mere results, well— obviously they would come.

The gods of football were walking amongst us.

Finally, the following week, a one-nil victory versus the brand-new Western Sydney Wanderers.

And the following week, another win, this time at home, against Perth.

At last, Sydney's season was off and racing.

Sadly this was a false dawn.

The following week, we were humiliated in Gosford by the Central Coast Mariners, a catastrophic seven-two loss in the pouring rain.

This was followed by a three-two loss at home to our arch rivals Melbourne Victory, and our season was officially a disaster.

We should have had that Melbourne game in the bag.

Sydney FC was dominant, leading two-nil well into the second half.

Del Piero was substituted in the sixty-fifth minute, and then it all started to go horribly wrong.

In the seventy-eighth minute, Melbourne's Andrew Nabbout scored.

In the eighty-sixth minute, Archie Thompson equalised for Melbourne.

On the sidelines, Sydney FC's coach Ian Crook kicked his chair away in frustration.

Then Nabbout runs in to score the winner in the first minute of stoppage time, appearing from nowhere amongst our seemingly frozen defenders to slam the ball home.

The goalkeeper barely moves.

It's like none of the Sydney players can quite believe what's happening.

It felt like some inexplicable curse had descended upon the stadium.

The very next morning, after only six matches in charge, Sydney FC's coach Ian Crook resigned.

PAIN AS ENTERTAINMENT

In his beautifully self-deprecating memoir *Fever Pitch*, author Nick Hornby explores his long-held and sometimes pathological obsession with English football team Arsenal.

From his perspective, football fandom offers a strange form of perverse pleasure, one that he became swallowed up by at a very young age.

Of his first experience at Arsenal's home ground of Highbury in 1968 as an eleven-year-old, he writes:

He reads from the book.

'It wasn't the size of the crowd that impressed me most, […] or the way that adults were allowed to shout the word 'WANKER!' as loudly as they wanted without attracting any attention. What impressed me most was just how much most of the men around me *hated*, really *hated*, being there. As far as I could tell, no-one seemed to enjoy, in the way that I understood the word, anything that happened during the entire afternoon. Within minutes of the kick-off there was real anger. ('You're a DISGRACE, Gould. He's a DISGRACE!' 'A hundred quid a week? A HUNDRED QUID A WEEK? They should give that to me for watching you.') As the game went on the anger turned into outrage, then seemed to curdle into sullen, silent discontent. […] [T]he natural state of the football fan is bitter disappointment, no matter what the score.

[…] Entertainment as pain was an idea entirely new to me, and it seemed to be something I'd been waiting for.'[7]

He puts the book down.

Unlike Hornby, I came to football fandom late.

But I could well understand the serious, passionate, morose obsession that he describes in this passage.

I have come to understand that football fandom is about *hope*, *loyalty* and *disappointment*.

You *hope* that things will turn around—that a new player signing, a new coach, a new training regime, or even a new team logo will magically make everything perfect again.

And with this hope driving you forward, you remain *loyal*.

And thereafter are ritually *disappointed*.

Again.

And with that, the cycle begins anew.

Nothing that can ever be done will ever really be good enough: despite a desperate, hopeful desire for perfection, everything ultimately disappoints.

And yet, I am compelled to return, again and again, desperately hoping that, despite all reasonable expectations to the contrary, I will be struck by a flash of wonder that makes it all worthwhile.

But sometimes, all of this hope doesn't really help.

Nick Hornby again:

'Each humiliating defeat […] must be borne with patience, fortitude and forbearance; there is simply nothing that can be done, and that is a realisation that can make you simply squirm with frustration.'[8]

MY HISTORY (SUCH AS IT IS) WITH SYDNEY FC

Despite some (largely inept) past participation in the sport, I had no real history with football.

As a twelve- and thirteen-year-old, I played for Greystanes Churches Football Club.

---

[7] Nick Hornby, *Fever Pitch*, 1992, pages 11–13. (Italics in original.)

[8] Nick Hornby, *Fever Pitch*, 1992, page 27.

For two seasons in the mid-eighties, Saturday mornings saw me being shuttled by my parents across the Western suburbs, all the way up to the lower Blue Mountains.

But I demonstrated no real flair for the game.

I was entirely oblivious to the old National Soccer League, and had been completely blind to the rich history of local football that had populated the landscape of my childhood.

I'd enjoyed the spectacle of past World Cups on television, but other than that, I had no particular passion for football.

I'd watched the occasional televised Socceroos match, including the 2006 World Cup matches.

I was in London for a conference at the time, and so had the slightly surreal experience of watching Australia versus Brazil in a Portuguese pub in East London with a couple of Australian academics.

Surrounded by Brazil jerseys, and with our team clearly outclassed, we started cheering every time Australia touched the ball.

It was fun, good-natured, and had just the right amount of beer.

I came to football fandom inauspiciously.

June 2007 was a strange time.

Everything in my life seemed to pause.

I finished a teaching contract at the University of NSW, and I finally submitted my doctoral thesis to examiners.

A month or so earlier, my girlfriend of the past five years had informed me that she needed a change.

She wanted more from her life, and I wasn't going to be able to help her be the person that she felt she needed to be.

To be honest, I've said things like this to other people in the past, but it was pretty brutal to be on the receiving end.

She was a writer, and post-breakup I found that I had appeared in one of her stories as a background character—referred to only as 'the man I no longer loved'.

It's like the comments section on newspaper articles—you should never read these things, but you just can't help yourself.

Anyway, suffice to say, it was a strange period in my life.

Both the now-ex-girlfriend and the PhD had been five-year projects, and both were now done and dusted.

I now had to sit and wait six months or so to find out whether or not the PhD would pass. So, perhaps unsurprisingly, in June 2007 I found myself at a little bit of a loose end.

Whilst in this odd little limbo, I was reading the newspaper one day, and I saw an insert about season passes for Sydney FC.

As I still had a valid student card, membership was really cheap— about sixty dollars for a Silver membership as I recall—that's a season pass with a reserved seat, very similar to the Black membership I would get with the Wanderers five years later (which cost me two hundred and fifty dollars, by the way).

I thought—why not?

I needed something new in my life, and the universe offered me football.

He puts on his 2007/2008 Sydney FC member's hat.

In that first year, I attended the football alone.

I would nod and smile at my new football neighbours, but we never developed much of a relationship beyond basic recognition. No first name introductions, just occasional disgruntled mutterings about the coach's tactical decisions or the competence of individual players.

We were all just intent on watching the game.

And for me, well, I was trying to work out who these people on the field were, what their stories were, and what the hell was going on.

I didn't plan on becoming a football fan.

Which perhaps explains why my team is Sydney FC.

After all, who would *plan* to become so obsessed with such a continually unsatisfying team?

A team that promises so much, and delivers, well, whatever it feels like on the day in question?

I became a fan, not necessarily because I fell in love with the game— it's too frustrating to realistically describe this kind of fandom as 'love'.

Instead, football became an ever-deepening obsession running in the background of my life, filling a gap that I hadn't quite realised was there.

For me, Sydney FC the team, like Sydney the city, offers a certain kind of pathological love—something I cling to despite knowing that having it will bring me nothing good.

SEASON NINE, GAME TWO

Jumping forward in time again. Back to Season Nine.

Friday, first November 2013.

Western Sydney Wanderers versus Adelaide United.

When inside the stadium, I strike up a conversation with my Bay forty-three, Row N neighbour, Andrew.

Originally I had misheard him, and for some reason thought that his name was Peter.

Anyway, his name is actually Andrew, and he and his family have season passes.

He's more of a rugby league guy, he says.

He tells me that his family has a membership with the Parramatta Eels NRL team, and how he loves rugby league.

But he loves the atmosphere at Wanderland more, and so has got very into football.

It helps that his wife thinks that Wanderers defender Jerome Polenz is hot.

That's Jerome Polenz, by the way.

> *He points at a picture of Polenz on the wall behind him.*

Hot.

Actually, throughout the season Andrew regularly jokes about his wife's fondness for Polenz.

One game later in the season, when Polenz doesn't play (injury or suspension, I can't remember which), Andrew remarks that it's good that his wife wasn't able to come to the game tonight, as she'd be upset not to see her 'boyfriend' on the field.

Anyway, Andrew works as a technician for a company that makes machines used in industrial packaging. So he has to travel a bit to service and install machines.

The family always has a generous supply of snacks to get everyone through the game—peanuts, fruit, cakes, *pastizzi*.

Often they share some with me.

Which is nice.

Andrew was very impressed that I knew what *pastizzis* were.

Apparently *pastizzis* are Maltese (I didn't know that), as is Andrew's heritage.

I remember, apropos of nothing, that there were quite a few Maltese families who lived nearby back in Greystanes.

Both parents and the two kids (a boy and girl—I never learn their names) all have Wanderers jerseys.

In fact, I'm amazed how many people of all sorts of different shapes and sizes are wearing red and black jerseys at the stadium.

Later I find out that the demand for merchandise was partly driven by scarcity—in the early days there weren't enough available to satisfy demand, and so every new batch of jerseys sold out straight away.[9]

I was curious as to whether or not Andrew's kids would attend tonight, given it was a Friday night rather than a Sunday afternoon, but sure enough, they were all there, singing along with the chants.

I admit to them that I really *am* a Sydney FC fan (just in case it hadn't been obvious from the previous game), but am also genuinely interested in watching the Wanderers play.

'The games don't clash!' I say truthfully, 'I can watch a game almost every week.'

I'm a little earlier to the game today, and notice the police at the stadium more.

---

[9]   According to John Stensholt and Shaun Mooney's 'Kit supplier Nike had forecast that the club would sell 10,000 home jerseys for the full year, but even before Christmas the club and other retailers had run out of stock.' (*A-League: The Inside Story of the Tumultuous First Decade*, 2015, page 220) Just to put that in context—that's a whole year of estimated sales in less than four months.

They are *very* present.

Tonight's game starts with a presentation of a ceremonial cheque for fifteen thousand dollars from the RBB to bushfire relief, a donation matched by Wanderers sponsor NRMA, and topped up by the local meeting place of the RBB, the Woolpack Hotel, with another three thousand dollars.

It's a lovely gesture, and paints a very different picture of Western Sydney's fans than has been appearing in the media.

If some of the media coverage is to be believed, the RBB are all tattooed violent gang members, and that assaults at and around matches are commonplace.

These are stories without any basis in anything that might be described as a 'fact', but you know, the not-so-subtle message is that soccer equals scary ethnic types, and good Aussie families should be worried.

Anyway.

It's an exciting game.

Western Sydney are all over Adelaide at the start.

Some great chances and near misses.

A couple of cards.

But it ends nil-all at the half-time break.

Against the run of play, Adelaide score in the fifty-fourth minute.

There's a strong offside shout, but the goal is given.

Suddenly energised, Adelaide repeatedly threatens to score again.

The red and black crowd tries to will their team to victory, and their chants get louder.

Join in if you know this one, Wanderers fans. Hands in the air.

> *He lifts both arms above his head.*

COME ON, YOU WANDERERS!

> *He claps twice and lifts his arms up again.*

COME ON, YOU WANDERERS!

> *He claps twice and lifts his arms up again.*

WE'LL ALWAYS LOVE YOU, NEVER BETRAY YOU!

COME ON, YOU WANDERERS!

> *He claps twice and lifts his arms up again.*

COME ON, YOU WANDERERS!

> *He claps twice and lifts his arms up again.*

COME ON, YOU WANDERERS!

> *He claps twice and lifts his arms up again.*

WE'LL ALWAYS LOVE YOU, NEVER BETRAY YOU!
COME ON, YOU WANDERERS!

> *He claps twice.*

Momentum switches, and Western Sydney fire shot after shot at Eugene Galekovic, the Adelaide goalkeeper.

Finally, Western Sydney's striker Tomi Juric scores a cracker.

A second goal fifteen minutes later seals it, though not without a few late scares.

It's a thrilling match.

I worry about how Sydney FC is going to deal with Adelaide—their passing and ball movement is pretty dazzling.

I have to leave slightly before the final whistle to get to work.

I'm meant to start work at the Opera House at nine-thirty p.m., so my partner Suzie thinks I'm mad to be going to a seven-thirty p.m. football match in Parramatta.

She's right.

I am of course quite late for work that night.

In the absence of the streaming crowds I notice the police positioning more—they're massed behind the signage at the back of the RBB, with twenty or more that I can see wearing riot gear, minus the plastic shields and helmets.

And up on the hilltop there's a cavalry detachment—four police horses in formation, just waiting.

It's a striking image, almost from another era.

Except for the high-vis vests.

And the fact that one policeman is checking something on his phone, his face lit slightly by its glow.

FOOTBALL FAMILY

Jump backing in time again.

After my student card expired in 2008, my Sydney FC membership became much more expensive.

I'd had an okay time attending the games, but wasn't entirely sure that I was sufficiently hooked to stump up some big-ish bucks.

Well, big-*er* bucks.

I umm-ed and ahh-ed about renewing, but then a unique solution presented itself.

My then-housemate's girlfriend Therese was also a Sydney FC fan, and she had worked out a good rort.

At the time, you could purchase a Family membership, supposedly for two adults and two kids. But in reality, they just gave you four passes.

So I joined her 'football family' for a few years.

It was much, much cheaper than a full-price season pass.

They've closed that loophole now, just so you know.

Which is a shame.

We saw good games and rubbish games.

Games that I can't remember at all.

We saw the revolving door of Sydney coaches—Branko Culina, then John Kosmina, then Vítězslav Lavička, then, ever-so-briefly, Ian Crook. And then came our latest attempt to turn results around, Frank Farina.

In early 2012, after the end of a season where Sydney FC had played another year of pretty boring football and had failed to progress in the finals series for the second year running, I became intrigued by talk of the new team being formed in Western Sydney.

I liked what I was hearing—fan forums where the club actually seemed to be listening to what people wanted? Crazy idea!

I liked the designs and the colours that were being proposed—red, black and white.[10]

---

[10] Even though I will always associate red, black and white with the long-defunct North Sydney Bears rugby league club.

The logo felt like a real football club, not the soulless corporate design of Sydney FC's badge.

I mean, the dominant feature of Sydney FC's badge is a soccer ball—like we need a ball on the badge so we remember that that it's a football team?[11]

But back to mid-2012.

I put it to my football family.

Rather than punish ourselves for another season, why don't we become foundation members of this new club?

Especially now that they've closed the Family Pass loophole and it's going to cost us all more?

It was of course a stupid question.

The other couple in our football family lived in Randwick, only one suburb away from Moore Park, the home stadium for Sydney FC.

They had precisely zero interest in travelling out to Parramatta every fortnight.

But it wasn't simply the extra travel involved.

Switching teams is an impossible thing to seriously contemplate.

One can't just *choose* to *change* football clubs.

As Nick Hornby writes in *Fever Pitch*, football loyalty 'was not a moral choice like bravery or kindness; it was more like a wart or a hump, something you were stuck with'[12].

We were stuck with it.

We signed up as Sydney FC members for another year.

Okay, this chant is for the Sydney FC side of the audience.

I'll do it once, and anyone who knows it join in. Then we'll do it a second time with everyone.

WE ARE SYDNEY!

---

[11] As a side note—I attended a Sydney FC members' forum in March 2016, and Sydney FC's management started to discuss a logo update. Members were genuinely thrilled by this idea. Given that we weren't able to discuss our frustrations with on-field strategies and tactics, the debate around the nature of the potential new logo was the most animated part of the night.

[12] Nick Hornby, *Fever Pitch*, 1992, page 27.

He claps.

THE FAMOUS SYDNEY FC!

He claps.

WE'RE FROM THE HARBOUR CITY!

He claps.

THE BOYS IN BLUE FROM MOORE PARK ROAD!
Now everyone, join in!
WE ARE SYDNEY!

He claps.

THE FAMOUS SYDNEY FC!

He claps.

WE'RE FROM THE HARBOUR CITY!

He claps.

THE BOYS IN BLUE FROM MOORE PARK ROAD!
One more time!
WE ARE SYDNEY!

He claps.

THE FAMOUS SYDNEY FC!

He claps.

WE'RE FROM THE HARBOUR CITY!

He claps.

THE BOYS IN BLUE FROM MOORE PARK ROAD!
WE ARE SYDNEY!

He signals a halt.

SEASON NINE, GAME FOUR

Jumping forward again.
Season Nine, Round eleven.
Monday, twenty-third December 2013.
Western Sydney Wanderers versus Central Coast Mariners.

I was a few hours early to this game, and so, in a very half-hearted and very late attempt at Christmas shopping, I wandered through Westfield Parramatta for a bit.

Everywhere there were shoppers in Wanderers shirts, but I did spot one lone woman in Mariners yellow.

Wandering around the shopping centre, I happened past Dymocks, and thought I might purchase a gift for Suzie's father.

After selecting the newest Tom Clancy novel, I joined the long queue to pay.

It was a long queue.

Upon finally reaching the counter, I noticed next to the register a large pile of Alessandro Del Piero's newly-updated autobiography, *Playing On: My Life On and Off the Field*.

I began a conversation with the salesperson about an interest in reading it, although I couldn't purchase it then as I expected that I would probably receive it as a Christmas gift.

(I didn't by the way. I had to buy it for myself later.)

She was somewhat confused.

Despite wearing sky blue, I *was* also clearly wearing a Western Sydney Wanderers member's lanyard, and the book features Del Piero in a very prominent Sydney FC jersey.

'You wouldn't be interested in that, I wouldn't think,' she says to me.

'But I'm interested in football. And he's a legendary footballer. He's amazing to watch. I'm headed over to Pirtek Stadium to watch the football now.'

'Oh, I could never go down *there*,' she replies.

'I'd be too scared—it's so violent!'

On that strange note, I left the shopping centre and followed the parade of happy smiling families in red and black jerseys to the stadium.

The Wanderers win again, two-nil.

SUBURBAN TERRORISTS

If you read the dominant media narratives about football in Australia, going to the football *does* seem like an extremely scary thing to do.

I've never found that to be the case myself, but the stigma remains.

And so, it seems that sometimes football fans find themselves treated as thugs, as hooligans, as wannabe criminals, without having to actually commit a crime.

The *Daily Telegraph*'s Rebecca Wilson suggested that soccer violence was an 'increasing menace'.[13]

Alan Jones linked football fans to terrorism in a discussion of alleged fan violence and asked, 'Is this like terrorism in Paris?'[14]

Herald Sun journalist Susie O'Brien deemed allegedly antisocial football fans as being 'little more than suburban terrorists'.[15]

But it wasn't only the media making such links.

Years earlier, back in 2009, the FFA (that's the Football Federation Australia, the national governing body for the game) engaged private security company Hatamoto to provide 'in-house security management support'.

Among their other clients, Hatamoto advises government departments on dealing with terrorism threats, so the fit with football fans seemed somewhat odd.

Undercover Hatamoto agents for several years attended games, filmed so-called 'troublemakers', and worked with the FFA to develop a list of people who should be banned from attending matches.

Some of these people committed illegal acts, and were prosecuted by police.

But many of them were never even accused of anything.

They were simply banned without being told why, shown no evidence, and given no right of appeal.

When pressed to explain a ban without recourse to evidence or appeal, the FFA stated in an email to one banned fan that:

'Please be advised that Football Federation Australia (FFA) is not a

---

[13] Rebecca Wilson, 'Don't believe the PR hype. Western Sydney must weed out criminal element', *Daily Telegraph,* January 3, 2014.

[14] Sebastian Hassett, 'Broadcaster Alan Jones compares A-League arrests to 'terrorism in Paris', *Sydney Morning Herald,* November 23, 2015.

[15] Susie O'Brien, 'Australian soccer fans shouldn't be supporting banned thugs', *Herald Sun,* November 30, 2015.

government agency and, as such, the obligation to adhere to the rules of procedural fairness and natural justice does not apply to our organisation. For this reason, FFA will not consider any appeal.'[16]

POLICING STRATEGIES

It's Tuesday, third November 2015.

A Senate Committee meets in Parramatta, to discuss, among other things, the policing strategies adopted for Wanderers games.

Here's testimony from the day's first witness, Police Assistant Commissioner Denis Clifford:

'I have been a police officer for forty-four years and have experience with crowd violence and public disorder associated with sporting events, demonstrations and other events such as the Cronulla riots and the Macquarie Fields riots and violence associated with the Canterbury Bulldogs some ten years ago.

'I recently met with the CEO of the Western Sydney Wanderers, officials of the FFA and management from Pirtek Stadium to express my concerns and my fears that it was only a matter of time before someone was seriously injured or killed as a result of the behaviour of some of the supporters. I raised a number of safety issues, including overcrowding in the stadium's northern seating area; supporters standing in and blocking the aisles; standing and jumping on seats; foul, vulgar, inciteful chants too disgusting to repeat here; and the unlawful use of flares.

'For the record, I enjoy most sports. I enjoy watching a game of soccer and find the chants and coordinated movements of the Western Sydney Wanderers fans entertaining and good for the sport. However, in my time as a player and spectator and as a coach of many junior sporting teams, I know the things that turn people away from healthy sport are violence, foul and abusive language, and risk to safety. The events that occurred prior to, during and after the recent game between Western Sydney Wanderers and Sydney FC, in my opinion, took things to a new

---

[16] Fadi Bushara, Red and Black Bloc, *Committee Hansard, Economic References Committee, Personal Choice and Community Impacts*. 3 November 2015, page 31.

low. I particularly refer to the ignition of numerous flares both inside and outside the stadium; the brawling between fans; and the damage to seating and the seating railings.

'You may have others appear here today before you to talk about how good the Western Sydney Wanderers have been for the game of football and, in particular, the City of Parramatta. I would agree with them, but we all must do as much as we can to stamp out the type of behaviour that I have just outlined before a tragedy is on our hands, such as a death or multiple deaths. Finally, I am concerned about the culture with some elements of the Western Sydney Wanderers fans. One only has to go to the RBB website, where you will see images that are, to me, most confronting and concerning. In a couple of images, there is a young child with a balaclava, carrying a flare and a loudhailer. As I say, to me—and to any reasonable person, I would suggest—they are confronting and very concerning.'[17]

The Stage Manager holds up an iPad with '2' on it.

Okay, the fourth official has declared that there shall be a minimum of two minutes time added on.

During later questioning, the assumptions that underpin Commissioner Clifford's statement were pretty comprehensively unravelled, especially his attempt to imply that football fan cultures necessarily equate with violence. Also strongly challenged was his view that policing strategies for football need to demonstrate a clear show of force.

Later, witnesses to the Senate Inquiry pretty passionately debunk this notion, noting that aggressive policing is regularly the cause of so-called 'violent' incidents, and that more appropriate stadium designs—including removing seats in the active supporter areas, will prevent potential damage and injuries.

As RBB member Fadi Bushara noted in his testimony:

---

[17] Assistant Commissioner Denis Clifford, Commander, North West Metropolitan Region, New South Wales Police Force, *Committee Hansard, Economic References Committee, Personal Choice and Community Impacts*. 3 November 2015, pages 1–2.

'Western Sydney does unite the people of the West and that is
nowhere more evident than in the RBB […] in terms of different
races, religions and even cultures. People are surprised—they say,
'How can you have people of Croatian background and people
of Serbian background together?' That all goes out the window
because nobody thinks like that; people are just there to support
the team. But it becomes very difficult for us to do so when we
feel there is always someone watching over our back or if people
feel intimidated. It is just natural to feel that way, and this is
happening regularly—more and more. It is facilitated by police.
There is just a stigma around the RBB. When people hear the word
'RBB' they think, 'Here we go—troublemakers, vigilante group',
call it what you will. It is an unfair tag that has been put on us.
Straightaway there is this perception, and this is what the police
follow. […] [D]o they target specific troublemakers? They do not.
They have a blanket approach; they say, 'RBB is here, off we go'.
Usually it is, 'Oh, we need ten police officers at this game,' but for
RBB, 'We need forty-five'. So it is always exaggerated. The media
always jumps on this as well. They like to sensationalise things
[…] It is always the case. We do what we do. We support the team:
we are active and we are vibrant—flags, colours, chanting and
marching. This is the attraction for a lot of people to this club.'[18]

The sound of a whistle blowing three times.

Okay!
That's half-time, everyone.
See you back in twenty minutes.

END OF ACT ONE

---

[18] Fadi Bushara, Red and Black Bloc, *Committee Hansard, Economic
References Committee, Personal Choice and Community Impacts.*
3 November 2015, pages 26–27.

ACT TWO

SPLIT YOURSELF IN HALF?

Hi, everyone, glad you made it back safely.

Is everyone back in their correct seats?

No half-time changes of allegiance?

No?

Great. Let's kick off the second half.

It's Season Nine, Round Fourteen.

Saturday, eleventh January 2014.

Western Sydney Wanderers versus Sydney FC.

The fifth Sydney derby.

I'm walking along Victoria Road, North Parramatta, in a huge, happily mixed crowd of sky blue and red/black.

I thought that it was appropriate to wear a Sydney FC away jersey today.

> *He removes his jacket to reveal his 2008/2009 Sydney FC away jersey.*

Just for fun I tracked this down on eBay—a 2008/2009 Sydney FC away jersey.

This was the final season that Tony Popovic, now the Wanderers coach, played for Sydney FC.

So I thought that it might be funny to get 'Popovic' and his old number 'six' put on the back.

There was a football store down the road from my house in Marrickville that probably could have done it for me, but by the time I got around to actually walking down there to get a quote, the business had closed down.

Bugger.

Anyway, I'm walking along Victoria Road, North Parramatta, toward the stadium, and this really huge Pacific Islander guy in a Wanderers jersey notices that I am wearing both a Sydney FC jersey and a red Wanderers member lanyard.

He does a double take, and then says to me, with genuine puzzlement:

'What do you do? Split yourself in half?'

We smile and share a couple of jokes about our respective teams.

The crowd all around us is in really excellent spirits.

The evening is warm, the weather is gorgeous, and all of us—sky blue and red and black—are really looking forward to the game.

Even the police doing crowd control seem happy today as they stop traffic to let thousands of us cross O'Connell Street.

Unfortunately, the media had a somewhat different perspective on this happy crowd.

The previous week, the *Daily Telegraph*'s Rebecca Wilson had written another article attacking the supposedly 'dangerous' Western Sydney Wanderers fans as being part of a violent so-called 'gang culture'.

'So what is it about this that makes my skin crawl?' she wrote.

'Why do I feel extremely uncomfortable when I see the so-called RBB in full voice at an A-League game, replete with a lot more than happy ditties and bonhomie? Certain fans who boast that they are RBB members hide their faces behind masks, rip hundreds of seats out of the stands so they can stand where they choose and smuggle flares into grounds despite a security presence that far outweighs most football games in Australia. Authorities desperately grappling with the increasing menace of a core group of fans have no answer to the trouble.'[19]

In response to this published provocation, before the kick-off the RBB display an enormous three-part banner.

I've had a replica made for you guys in the Western bloc of the audience to display.

Starting from the top row, and from the stage right end of the row—that's my right by the way.

Pull out the banner and pass the edge along.

---

[19] Rebecca Wilson, 'Don't believe the PR hype. Western Sydney must weed out criminal element', *Daily Telegraph,* January 3, 2014.

Great.

Hold it stretched out.

Fantastic.

Now the middle row.

Same procedure.

Roll it out, and pass the edge across.

Now the bottom rows, same process.

For those of you holding the sign who cannot read it, it says:

'REBECCA WILSON:

WORRY ABOUT AN RBT

NOT THE RBB!'

In case anyone doesn't get it, this is a reference to the fact that she was
   previously charged with a drink-driving offence.

Now some audience members might think that this anecdote is in bad
   taste, given that Rebecca Wilson died late last year.

I make no judgement about her character.

I have no knowledge of her as a person.

But it remains indisputable that amongst a group of journalists known
   for their regular negative commentary about football, she became
   the most notorious.

This escalated after her so-called 'Soccer Shame File' article in
   November 2015 for the *Daily Telegraph*, in which she published
   the names and photographs of one hundred and ninety-eight fans
   confidentially banned by the FFA for alleged bad behaviour.

At least one of these men claimed to have been sacked from his job as
   a consequence of this news story.

Legal actions are continuing to develop.

Anyway, despite the palpable media desire for scandal, in this second
   Sydney derby of Season Nine, the crowd is well-behaved, friendly
   and has a good time.

Western Sydney wins again, one-nil.

I smile a lot, and all of these smiles are genuine.

I don't need to split myself in half.

THE TROUBLE-SEEKING GAZE

I'm back at Parramatta two years later for the same fixture, the second Sydney derby of Season Eleven, January sixteen, 2016.

My partner Suzie has come along for her first visit to Wanderland.

There are police everywhere as we approach the stadium, far more than I've seen at previous derby matches.

Someone in the Parramatta Local Area Command clearly wants an impressive show of force.

I hope that no-one anywhere else in Western Sydney needs police assistance tonight!

Suzie and I sit in the front row of the first level of the eastern grandstand, above The Cove, but with a good view of the RBB as well.

The game is just underway, and two police walk up the stairs next to our seats.

They stop and linger at the top of the staircase, perhaps to monitor the crowd.

But rather than stay at the edge of the staircase where they won't obstruct anyone's view, they chose to move sideways and stand directly in front of us.

And I don't mean this figuratively.

They stood directly in front of us, totally blocking our view of the field.

I politely and reasonably ask if they could take a couple of steps to their right so we might be able to see the game.

One of the policemen turns to me and almost snarls:

'Why don't you go sit somewhere else?'

I start to suggest that these are reserved seats, and perhaps we have a right to be where we were—it's not true by the way, we were supposed to be in the Sydney active area, but couldn't fit in.

But the policeman doesn't know that, and sure as hell we're not going to volunteer this information.

The cop just stares at me.

There's a short pause.

I can sense that he wants an excuse to escalate the situation.

His mate looks at us, and perhaps realising for the first time that they might be in the wrong, or simply that they're dealing with a couple, not just some mouthy bloke.

He mutters something inaudible to his partner, and they move on without another word.

I can't help but wonder what might have happened had I been by myself.

Shortly afterwards, with the help of the stadium staff, we move to another section as well.

I feel far safer seated in the middle of a row of enthusiastic Wanderers supporters than I do under the trouble-seeking gaze of local law enforcement.

I get into some enjoyable banter with the group of Wanderers fans next to us, and on the field Sydney FC holds off wave after wave of attacks.

We're defending deep, with the entire team behind the ball.

It's not pretty, but against all expectations it's working.

And then, against the run of play, we score from a set piece play— with Jacques Faty rising to head home from a corner.

Finally we succumb to an equaliser—a very impressive Dario Vidosic strike.

It wasn't really a surprise—a goal had been coming for a while.

The guy sitting next to me says:

'Look, you seem like a nice guy, so don't take this personally. But if we score a winner late in the match, I'm going to have to throw beer over you.'

I smile and pull up my hood.

They don't score.

Instead, there's a late goalmouth scramble, and Sydney FC's Shane Smeltz pounces on a loose ball.

He smashes it into the back of the net.

We hold on for the win.

Not sure we deserved it, but nevertheless it's a very satisfying victory.

Even my potential beer-throwing neighbour congratulates me, graciously conceding Sydney's superior tactics on this occasion.

The following day one newspaper headline calls it 'The Great Western Highway Robbery'.

Happy times.

Two years earlier, back in Season Nine, there were very few such happy times for Sydney FC fans.

'WE WANT FARINA GONE'

It's Boxing Day, 2013, and I'm on the train home after yet another disappointing Sydney FC loss at home.

On the field, Del Piero looks more and more like he's going through the motions; like he'd rather be anywhere else but here.

It feels disrespectful to say this of a football god, but let's face it.

He's starting to look his age.

He can't be expected to hold the team up all by himself.

'Keep calm and kick it to Del Piero!' isn't really a very sustainable strategy.

Frank Farina, our then-coach, has done okay in stabilising a club that seemed for a while to be in freefall.

But form has dipped again.

The fans are getting really restless.

We've suffered a lot, and surely there must be some limits to our future suffering.

Surely.

Farina is talking a good talk and putting a brave face on it, but hashtag 'farinaout' has been getting a *lot* of traction on social media.

No-one in the Sydney FC camp is happy, and Farina is running out of time to turn the ship around.

The past few months have had ups and downs for Sydney FC.

At home, back in early December, we won a pretty scrappy game against Melbourne Heart, a game which featured another magic moment from Del Piero.

He hadn't seemed very present in this game, but he suddenly came
   alive near the half-way line.

He takes off on a mazy run, stepping, stepping, stepping, dancing
   around defenders, and then *bang*!

He shoots, he scores!

We're on top for the rest of the half, but after the break, Melbourne
   brings Harry Kewell on. Kewell, despite being very far from in
   his prime (like Del Piero to be fair), starts causing us all sorts of
   problems.

A short time later there's a handball call in the Sydney FC penalty area.

REFEREE! C'MON! SIR!

I mean, you could argue, as the crowd did vociferously, that this was
   a case of ball to hand rather than hand to ball, but the ref points to
   the spot and Harry Kewell steps up to take the penalty.

All of us in the crowd collectively hold our breath.

Kewell places the ball, sets himself, and kicks.

It's a terrible, terrible miss-hit, and the ball flies miles wide of the goal.

All of us in the crowd laugh and shout, partly in derision, partly in
   relief.

Video of that penalty shot will undoubtedly be watched and re-watched
   for years to come. Look it up on YouTube.

Sydney holds on for the win.

Anyway, I'm on the train on Boxing Day, 2013, and we've just been
   smashed again by Brisbane.

They absolutely killed us this time, five-two.

An utterly embarrassing scoreline.

And to rub salt into the wounds, former Sydney FC player Dimitri
   Petratos has scored a hat-trick against us.

It wasn't just the loss, it was the pathetic-ness of the display.

It was like no-one on the field was either on the same team, or actually
   wanted to be there.

Something was clearly wrong, perhaps in the dressing room, perhaps
   in the boardroom.

Perhaps both.

I was on the train home after this miserable defeat.

It's crowded, and I'm standing in the vestibule area in my Sydney FC gear.

Apropos of nothing, this middle-aged paint-splattered tradie just starts chatting to me.

He's friendly, and says he used to play with Sydney FC's coach Frank Farina.

I don't ask where and when, and he doesn't offer.

But he says to me, out of nowhere:

'Frankie's problem was that he always did like a bit of a drink.'

There have been lots of jibes directed at Farina over the past few months based around this theme, and it's true that he was sacked from a previous coaching job at Queensland Roar several years ago due to a drink-driving offence.

He's clearly under a lot of pressure, and the jibes aren't helping.

There's a sense of genuine crisis.

After the evisceration by Brisbane, things get a little better, then a lot, lot worse.

Away, we have an unbelievable game on Australia Day, 2014, smashing our archrivals Melbourne Victory five-nil.

But I wasn't there to see that.

So it's like it didn't really happen.

A couple of weeks later was probably the lowest point of a season filled with low points.

It's Round Eighteen, Saturday, eighth February 2014.

Sydney FC versus Adelaide United.

Pre-match, The Cove display a giant banner.

I've had a replica made for you guys in the Sydney FC bloc of the audience to display.

It's smaller than the last one, so it's just one piece.

Starting from the middle row, and from the stage left end of the row— that's my left, by the way.

Pull out the banner and pass the edge along.

Great.

Hold it stretched out.

Fantastic.

For those of you holding the sign who cannot read it, it says:

'WE WANT FARINA GONE!'

It's accompanied by a message in Cyrillic to Sydney FC's Russian owner David Traktovenko to sack both the coach and the club's management team.

When stadium staff tries to remove the banners and eject the protestors, it triggers a mass walkout from The Cove.

The stadium falls eerily silent.

Adelaide scores once, then again.

Our team is in disarray on the pitch.

Nothing comes together.

Two half-time substitutions, and the experienced players Nicky Carle and Matt Thompson enter the field.

They have a brief on-field huddle, and then decide, against the coach's instructions, to swap positions.

Farina is justifiably furious.

Neither of these players make much of an appearance for the remainder of the season.

Someone in the crowd empties a beer over Farina's head as he sits on the sideline.

> *He empties a beer onto the ground.*

Adelaide romp to victory, three-nil.

And that scoreline was highly flattering to Sydney.

To say that this game was a disappointment is a severe understatement.

I'm a Sydney FC fan—I've had years to become accustomed to disappointment.

This game was something else.

This game caused trauma to the soul.

A SOUL?

Afterwards, revered football journalist Les Murray conducted an extended interview with Sydney FC's chairman, Scott Barlow.

Les Murray asked:

'There are claims out there in the media and among the public that
    Sydney FC is in some kind of crisis. […] Critics are claiming that
    the club struggles with having an identity. Or a soul. What's your
    response?'

Scott Barlow replied:

'I don't agree with that. For me, our identity is very clear. Sydney,
    the city, is an iconic city of the world. It is a beautiful city, it is
    an ambitious city. And Sydney FC needs to represent all of these
    things. In my opinion the best football clubs in the world—their
    identity represents where they are from, and what better place
    to represent than Sydney? So everything that Sydney is, to the
    rest of Australia and to the world, is what we want Sydney FC to
    represent. Now it's a big, bold, ambitious city, and that's what we
    want our club to be, and that's certainly what our strategy and our
    vision is for the club going forward.'[20]

They're nice words. Well-crafted words.

But they are difficult to feel passionate about.

Because they don't actually *mean* anything.

Two years later, at the member forum in March 2016, Scott Barlow
    said something very similar:

'The greatest football clubs in the world are a reflection of the city
    they represent. We are Sydney—big, bold, iconic. Sydney FC is a
    premium brand, an aspirational brand, an international brand.'[21]

Again, these are polished words, and they work well as part of a
    corporate marketing and business plan.

And certainly, the club has to be a well-managed business in order to
    keep the doors open.

I can appreciate that the club needs to recoup its investments.

Cover its costs.

Pay its staff.

I appreciate that the owner loses a lot of money keeping the club afloat.

I get all that.

---

[20] Interview between Les Murray and Scott Barlow, SBS, 28 February 2014.

[21] Scott Barlow at Sydney FC Members forum, Wednesday 9 March 2016.
    Forum held at ICC Theatrette, Drive Avenue, Allianz Stadium.

But I want clubs to be more than just businesses.

I want to be part of something bigger.

I want to connect with the *soul* that Les Murray asked about.

And you can't create a soul simply by throwing money around.

NATURAL BIRTH INTENSIVE

Back to Season Nine.

The third and final Sydney derby for the season was at Moore Park, and much to my disgust, I was unable to attend.

The match was on eighth March, 2014, a Saturday night.

At the time Suzie is pretty heavily pregnant, and so she had only attended a couple of Sydney FC home games all season.

With the baby due in about three weeks, this would almost certainly be her last game for a while.

But alas, it was not to be.

RPA—Royal Prince Alfred Hospital—where we were booked into for the birth, ran a series of pre-natal classes and information sessions, and being first-time and pretty apprehensive parents, we'd signed up for pretty much all of them.

Most of them were during the day, but the last class, entitled the 'Natural Birth Intensive', was scheduled for a Thursday night.

Fair enough—not everyone has flexible work hours.

All fine and good.

About a week before the class was due to run, we were advised that the midwife running it was no longer available at the scheduled time, and so there would a time change.

Again all good, our schedule was pretty flexible, and, I thought confidently, there's no way that they'd put it on a Saturday night.

No way.

Derby night was going to be fine.

Note to future self—in such a circumstance, never, ever, ever think such a thought ever again.

The *only* time the hospital was able to reschedule the class was Saturday night, from six p.m. until nine p.m.

Kick off for the derby was seven forty-five p.m.

There was no way in hell that this was going to work.

I tried to think of all sorts of quasi-reasonable excuses about why it was not super important that I attend this particular class, that Saturday night was a terrible time to learn about intervention-free birthing strategies.

But I knew that this would be doomed.

So, we're at the hospital talking about the stages and mechanics of labour, effective strategies for pain management—including a demonstration of how epidurals work.

If anyone is unfamiliar with these—it's a terrifyingly large needle that gets inserted into the spine in order to eliminate all sensation below the point of injection.

It's the kind of thing that sounds okay until you actually see what it looks like.

Kick-off over at Moore Park happens part-way through the first half of the class, and it takes every bit of willpower I possess not to compulsively check the Twitter stream on my phone.

I've been busted doing this at a few events in the past, you know, wedding receptions and the like.

It's never a good look.

Finally we get a tea-break, and whilst Suzie ducks off to the toilet I check my phone.

The score is nil-all.

Phew.

Still nil-all.

Maybe we can hold this together.

I manage to surreptitiously check my phone a few more times during the last bit of the class, as the scoreline remains even right up until half-time.

By the time the class ends, the second half is just underway.

Suzie is amenable to the idea of going down and watching the remainder of the second half at the Alfred Hotel, the pub down on Missenden Road near where we parked the car.

Great.

Another toilet break, and we can be on our way.

Moments later my Twitter feed explodes as Western Sydney score.

Bloody Shinji Ono again.

Then Twitter informs me that there's a penalty awarded against Sydney.

Shit. Shit. Shit. Shit. Shit. Shit. Shit.

I'm getting very anxious now—we need to get out of the hospital and in front of that screen *right now.*

After what feels like an age, we get to the pub.

It's pretty quiet for a Saturday, and the barman is very happy to change the channel so we can watch the match.

In the ten minutes or so that it's taken us to shuffle down the road, Sydney FC somehow has not only saved the penalty but also equalised.

No idea how that happened.

Some kind of divine intervention, no doubt.

It's clearly an edgy and intense game, and it was very stressful viewing.

Then, inexplicably, Wanderers defender Michael Beauchamp makes a calamitous error—a too-gentle, too-short pass back to his goalkeeper Ante Covic.

Sydney FC's Richard Garcia is standing right next to him, and leaps upon the gift of the loose ball, slotting it calmly into the net past the onrushing Covic.

Sydney FC two, Western Sydney Wanderers one.

Shortly afterwards, there's a heated dispute on the field between Sydney's Ali Abbas and Western Sydney's Brendon Santalab.

As more players come over, it looks like it could break out into an all-in brawl.

If I had been watching the game at the stadium I wouldn't have seen the close-ups of Abbas' face.

I wouldn't have seen how enraged he was at whatever had happened.

Abbas has always been a passionate player, but I've never seen him snap like this.

Sydney's giant central defender Sasha Ognenovski literally had to pick him up off his feet and drag him away.

Something out-of-the ordinary had clearly just happened.

But exactly *what* was unclear.

There's a very late penalty, which Abbas takes and scores.

Final score: Sydney three, Western Sydney one.

A dramatic end to a dramatic match.

After the final whistle, a sweat-drenched and still-emotional Ali Abbas was interviewed about the incident.

'We are not here to attack religion or culture, we are here to play football,' he said.

'I come from a different country, I respect everyone here. I should get it back. If I don't get it back, I'm going to attack. That's what happened. If people attack religion, if people attack culture—I'm against that. We need to stop that.'

Post-match, Sydney FC made a formal complaint about the alleged abuse, which Santalab flatly denied.

In the absence of any corroborating evidence, no action was taken.

But the sore festered.

Six months later, in November 2014, during the first Sydney derby of Season Ten, Ali Abbas was subjected to several very hard tackles by Wanderers players. The second of which, a forceful collision with Iacopo La Rocca, saw Abbas stretchered from the field.

Scans revealed tears in both his medial and anterior cruciate ligaments.

It was more than a year before he was able to play again.

I really struggle with racialised banter.

At the derby match at Parramatta in 2016, during my friendly banter with the Wanderers supporters all around me, I was happy to accept that Sydney FC striker Matt Simon had a reputation as a bit of a thug.

On the field, at least.

He's a big, hardworking, physically intimidating type, and must hold some sort of world record for the number of yellow cards accrued per minute played.

As I said at the time:

'He may be a thug, sure, but he's *our* thug. Kind of like Brendon Santalab for you guys.'

But I got increasingly uncomfortable with all of the Wanderers fans around me referring to Abbas as 'Ali Kebabs'.

Wanderers fans never forgave Abbas for publically suggesting that Santalab was a racist, and so when Abbas came on as a substitute late in this game it was to loud boos and jeers from the red and black crowd.

I don't mind the boos—every team has to have its own villains.

Like Melbourne Victory's coach Kevin Muscat.

Or striker Besart Berisha.

Players we love to hate.

So I can deal with boos.

But this was something else.

Despite all the rhetoric around the Wanderers' strength being driven by the cultural diversity of their fans, I heard Ali Abbas loudly and continuously mocked as Ali Kebabs, Ali Kebabs, Ali Kebabs.

'EAT SOME MORE KEBABS, ALI!'

All in the name of 'fun'.

Of this, I am not a fan.

A TEAM FOR ALL OF SYDNEY

This chant is for the Sydney side of the audience, and it's called 'Take Me to the Harbour'.

Join in if you know it, Sydney fans.

SYDNEY, SYDNEY, OH SYDNEY', SAID I,
I WILL STAND IN MOORE PARK TILL THE DAY I DIE,
TAKE ME TO THE HARBOUR, WAY DOWN BY THE SEA,
WHERE I WILL FOLLOW SYDNEY, SYDNEY FC.

Once more.

SYDNEY, SYDNEY, OH SYDNEY', SAID I,
I WILL STAND IN MOORE PARK TILL THE DAY I DIE,
TAKE ME TO THE HARBOUR, WAY DOWN BY THE SEA,
WHERE I WILL FOLLOW SYDNEY, SYDNEY FC.

Thanks, that's great.

Back in 2004, my father—a small 'c' conservative voter—quite liked then-Labor leader Mark Latham.

Which was pretty unusual—my dad wasn't really a Labor guy.

As far as I could tell, this wasn't about Latham's policies or platforms, and certainly not about Latham's personality. But rather it seemed driven by the idea that Latham, who grew up in Green Valley, south-west of Liverpool, publicly *hated* the North Shore.

As a lifelong resident of the Greater West, it made sense to my dad to hate the North Shore.

Not the *people* who lived on the North Shore.

Just the *idea* of the North Shore.

What the North Shore represented.

Affluence.

Power.

Undeserved privilege.

A hatred of the North Shore was a world view that my dad could empathise with.

To be fair, it's a pretty passive 'hatred'.

More of a mild resentment.

I've inherited a bit of that, though I acknowledge that it's a totally illogical world view.

I mean my relationship with the north side of Sydney is pretty much zero, so why should I care about them enough to resent them?

And yet, at particular moments, this sense of 'them' negatively affecting the daily lives of 'us' is palpable.

This resentment has a 'truthiness' (to use Stephen Colbert's term).

A sense of *feeling* true, regardless of whether it actually *is* true.

And the 'truthiness' of this sense of difference, separateness and division drives the passion of fans.

My team is better, stronger, greater, worthier, more exciting, more deserving and more hard-done-by than yours.

Not for many objectively measurable reasons.

But rather because I passionately believe this to be true.

Because this *feels* true.

Even when I hate it, my team is better than yours.

Because it's *my* team.

At the March 2016 member forum, Sydney FC's chairman Scott Barlow said that:

'We are a club for all of Sydney, with our heartland in Sydney's north, south, east and inner west.'

That's a pretty fractured heartland.

Only someone not *from* Sydney[22] could ever say that with a straight face.

In my experience of living in Sydney over the past forty-plus years, I've found that each of the areas that Barlow mentions have very little in common.

But in terms of membership metrics, he's correct.

Sydney FC's members *are* geographically spread all across Sydney.

Very few were from the eastern suburbs (nine per cent in 2016), so the east/west divide doesn't really make any sense.[23]

But the east/west division *feels* true.

It has truthiness.

But the idea that all of Sydney is the same—that all of the five-odd million people that live here have the same or even similar interests, outlooks, hopes and dreams is pretty questionable.

Like everywhere else, Sydney is a city shaped by divisions, by disconnections, by distastes or sometimes outright hostilities to those 'other' parts of the greater city—the parts of the city most alien to people like 'us'.

Whatever 'us' might mean.

So how can a football team 'belong' to everyone in a city like

---

[22] Scott Barlow grew up in Tasmania.

[23] For interest's sake, Sydney FC management stated at the Member Forum in March 2016 that nine per cent of members were from the eastern suburbs, twenty-two per cent were from the north, twenty-six per cent from the inner west and twenty-nine per cent from the south, the rest from 'other'.

Sydney?

Well, it can't.

And this was always the problem faced by Sydney FC.

Saying that you are a team for everyone in Sydney doesn't actually *make* you a team for everyone in Sydney.

No matter how much you might want that to be true.

WESTERN SYDNEY IS SOMEWHERE

As a Wanderers member in Season Nine, I receive a lot of fan communication. This mostly takes the form of emails from the club's communications team once or twice per week.

One thing I notice about these emails is that they don't talk much about who the club *is*.

Instead, they appear to focus on what the club *does*.

Unlike Sydney FC, the Wanderers don't need to obsess about identity. They just get on with the job.

It's pretty easy to understand why.

To paraphrase Bill Clinton: 'It's about the geography stupid!'

The Western Sydney Wanderers are from *somewhere*.

As much as Western Sydney is a huge and hugely mixed-up collection of suburbs, they share a sense that they've been doing it tough, that the rest of Sydney doesn't care about them or hasn't given them a fair share.

There's plenty of justification for this view—just look at the disparity in expenditure on public infrastructure between the inner city and the Greater West.

As someone who lived in Western Sydney for over twenty years, I understand this feeling of being ignored.

Of not feeling valued.

Of not being taken seriously.

Of not being noticed.

Of being an outsider.

These insecurities, both real and imagined, have fundamentally shaped my lived experience of this city.

Greystanes has very little in common with Fairfield and Blacktown
and Penrith and Campbelltown and Wentworthville and Parramatta
and Granville and Auburn and Merrylands and Guildford and
Yennora and Harris Park and Liverpool and all of the other
suburbs too numerous to mention.

Each of these suburbs have their distinct communities, their histories,
their challenges, their opportunities, their identities.

But they share a fundamental sense that they have been left behind
and forgotten by the rest of Sydney.

And the only time they get any attention is when something goes
wrong.

The formation of the Western Sydney Wanderers gave all of these
suburbs a shared something to be proud of.

Something that they could all belong to.

Something that could capture their hopes, imaginations and dreams.

Part of me wishes that they had existed at a time when they could
have been *my* team, and I could stand at the stadium holding up a
sign with my old postcode on it: 2145.

He holds up a sign with '2145' written on it.

At the first Sydney derby played at Allianz Stadium, Sydney FC's
home ground at Moore Park in December 2012, hundreds of
Wanderers fans held up signs with their postcodes on them.

As if to say:

Look at where we've come from!

You can't ignore us now.

You can't ignore us anymore.

As if to say:

We're all here.

See us.

Listen to us.

Treat our hopes and dreams and aspirations seriously.

Stop mocking us.

Stop belittling us.

Stop pretending we don't matter.

Stop pretending that we don't exist.

Stop pretending that we don't exist.

We're here.

We're proud of where we come from.

We're passionate.

We're together.

And together, we have power.

As a young member of the RBB once said to me:

'It's not about the competition. It's about showing that we're here—
    Western Sydney is in your face.'

Another chant now.

Western Sydney audience, join in if you know it. The tune is 'Bad
    Moon Rising'.

WE'RE FROM THE STREETS OF WESTERN SYDNEY,
HOME OF THE MIGHTY RBB!
RBB!
WE WILL FOLLOW YOU FOREVER,
WE WILL BE BY YOUR SIDE!

COME ON COME ON WANDERERS,
COME ON COME ON WANDERERS,
COME ON COME ON COME ON COME ON WANDERERS!
COME ON COME ON WANDERERS,
COME ON COME ON WANDERERS,
COME ON COME ON COME ON COME ON WANDERERS!

WE'RE FROM THE STREETS OF WESTERN SYDNEY,
HOME OF THE MIGHTY RBB!
RBB!
WE WILL FOLLOW YOU FOREVER,
WE WILL BE BY YOUR SIDE!

COME ON COME ON WANDERERS,
COME ON COME ON WANDERERS,
COME ON COME ON COME ON COME ON WANDERERS!
COME ON COME ON WANDERERS,
COME ON COME ON WANDERERS,
COME ON COME ON COME ON COME ON WANDERERS!

SHINJI ONO'S FINAL GAME

It's Saturday, fifth April 2014.

The last Wanderers home game of Season Nine.

Western Sydney Wanderers versus Brisbane Roar.

This will be Shinji Ono's final regular-season A-League match at Wanderland, so there are special plans afoot.

Reports in the media suggest that he was keen to continue for at least another year, but coach Tony Popovic, unsentimental as always, decides against offering him another contract.

And so it's the official farewell game for Shinji Ono, even though it won't actually be his last game in Wanderers colours.

Pre-match, the RBB display a fantastic Ono banner—with his face painted in the centre of a gigantic rising sun flag.

Throughout the stadium there are dozens of celebratory Shinji Ono banners of homemade manufacture and varying quality, including a whole bunch of giant re-branded Uno cards.

Uno. Ono. Get it?

To celebrate his jersey number, there are fireworks in the twenty-first minute—red explosions all around the stadium.

But the match doesn't pause.

Huge sections of the crowd put on simple cardboard masks with Shinji Ono's face on them. It's a pretty awesome sight.

Thousands of these masks were distributed at the entrance gates, but sadly I didn't arrive early enough to get one.

In the second half, the crowd starts to hold their phones in the air with the lights on, and thousands of twinkling stars appear against the gathering night.

The whole evening has the feel of a carnival.

It was a great match to watch, despite ending up as a one-all draw. It's an entertaining arm wrestle between the two best teams in the league this season.

I don't take many notes, but I do take a few good pictures.

Children, all around me.

Wearing Shinji Ono masks, excitedly waving flags, enthusiastically singing along to all the songs.

The passionately embittered middle-aged men a couple rows down from me and across the aisle.

Who grumbled all season long about every missed pass, every stumble, every mistimed tackle, every misplaced shot.

Who, every single time that there was anything even vaguely contentious, would vigorously appeal to the referee with heated cries of:

'SIR! SIR! C'MON, SIR!'

Tonight, even they are smiling.

There's magic in the air when the match ends, and we all spill happily out of the stadium gates and into the night.

I walk back across the Parramatta Pool carpark, across the river, past the entrance to Parramatta Park, and back to the train station for the ride back home.

I'll miss this.

I really will miss this.

SAINT TERRY

The following Sunday, thirteenth April 2014, is Sydney FC's final home game, playing against Perth Glory.

Our son Archie was born a couple of days previously, so life is a bit strange and exhausting at this moment in time.

So escaping to the football, if only for a couple of hours, was very welcome.

Before the match there's a farewell to Sydney FC foundation player Terry McFlynn, who is injured and can't play in this last match.

Terry does a lap of the field to a standing ovation from the crowd.

It's bittersweet seeing a hero of the club paraded at his final match wearing a suit and tie rather than boots and jersey.

The Cove display an enormous banner depicting him as 'Saint Terry' in a mock-stained glass window, carrying a staff and the Sydney Opera House safely under his arm.

They then lead the stadium in a rousing rendition of 'Hey, Terry Terry'.

Sydney fans, let's give this chant a red-hot go.

The lyrics are really really complex.

I'll demonstrate:

HEY, TERRY TERRY!

TERRY TERRY TERRY TERRY TERRY TERRY TERRY MCFLYNN!

Got it? Let's give it a go together.

Ready? One, two, three!

> *He chants along with the Sydney FC audience bloc.*

HEY, TERRY TERRY!

TERRY TERRY TERRY TERRY TERRY TERRY TERRY MCFLYNN!

Once more.

> *He chants along with the Sydney FC audience bloc.*

HEY, TERRY TERRY!

TERRY TERRY TERRY TERRY TERRY TERRY TERRY MCFLYNN!

That's great, thanks.

There's a lot at stake in this match.

If we win, Sydney is through into the finals.

Perth have nothing to play for—their season is over, with a finals berth out of reach.

But the league table is so tight in the middle that if Sydney loses, we could finish in seventh spot.

If we *lose*, and then Newcastle wins their match by more than two goals, we're out.

So we need to win.

Or at least draw.

No pressure.

So no-one is talking about the fact that this might be the last time we see Alessandro Del Piero at home in sky blue.

Talks about a contract extension are apparently ongoing, so there's no talk of farewells.

Not yet.

It's a scrappy, underwhelming match, filled with nerves.

Nothing really comes together, but then there's a beautiful strike from Sydney FC's Terry Antonis to open the scoring in the thirty-eighth minute.

A little sideways pass from Del Piero, then Antonis runs in and *smack!*

A rocket into the back of the net from about twenty metres out.

Thank God.

Then right at the end of the first half, our goalkeeper Vedran Janjetovic flaps his arms toward a lobbed-over corner kick, but can't get a hold of it.

Our defensive line has gone to sleep. Again.

Perhaps they're already looking forward to a bit of a break.

It seems that no-one notices Perth's Rostyn Griffiths standing amongst them.

The ball comes straight to him, and with all our defenders frozen, he taps it home.

One-all.

After the break it's more of the same.

Scrappy disconnections, narrow escapes, almost-magic moments.

Del Piero gets on the end of a lovely cross, but Perth's keeper makes a fantastic reflex save.

Then, right at the death, Sydney FC's Richard Garcia scores the winner.

Sydney FC is off to Melbourne for the first elimination final.

As I now have a two-week-old son, there's absolutely no way to even contemplate a trip down to Melbourne.

Pause.

Absolutely no way.

Pause.

Okay, so I did contemplate it.

But not very seriously.

It's not really a surprise to me that Sydney is eliminated at this first hurdle.

It's been that kind of year.

No more moments of magic, no last-second heroics.

No new contract for Del Piero.

No farewells.

Sydney FC's season is over, and coach Frank Farina is shown the door. A period of rebuilding commences.

POZNAN

At the eightieth minute of every Wanderers match, the whole stadium stands and does a shared routine called the Poznan.

It's named for the team that first started doing it in 1961—Lech Poznan in Poland. Fans from Lech Poznan call it the 'Grecque', but other teams who adopted it call it simply the Poznan.

Anyway, the action involves everyone in the stadium standing, turning away from the field, joining arms, and jumping up and down on the spot for about one minute.

Wanderers supporters do the Poznan in the eightieth minute of the game in order to commemorate the first recorded football match that took place in Western Sydney in 1880.

As it's now the eightieth minute, I'd like my Western Sydney audience comrades to stand and do the Poznan.

Everyone stand, turn away from the stage, join arms, and jump up and down on the spot for about one minute.

They do the Poznan for approximately one minute.

Thanks so much, everyone, that's fantastic.

You can all take a seat again.

In my year of visiting Wanderland, I decide not to join in the Poznan.

People jump up and down all around me, smiling, sharing a special moment together.

It felt a bit like taking communion in someone else's church—not really a respectful thing to do.

It's the only time in every match that I truly feel like an outsider, that this landscape does not and cannot belong to me.

Even though I happened to be born here.

SEASON NINE ENDS

In Season Nine, Western Sydney Wanderers ultimately reach the grand final, and thousands of fans travel up to Brisbane to paint Suncorp

Stadium red and black.

But luck does not favour the Wanderers, and they heartbreakingly lose in extra time.

The team channels their energies over the next year into the Asian Champions League, which, unbelievably and against all the odds, they win.

Truly amazing.

After so much success so quickly, I wonder what will happen when the inevitable happens—when the Wanderers become a club like all others. When they become frustrating, inconsistent, unlucky, and frequently disappointing.

Like they are now, in 2017.

It's easy to deal with disappointment when that's the majority of what you've been given over many years.

But when you're young and you've had the gift of such a glorious fairytale beginning?

Well, I imagine that slumping back to Earth might be somewhat harder to take.

We'll see.

NOW (AT TIME OF WRITING)

Jumping forward in time two years.

April tenth, 2016.

Sydney FC versus Perth Glory.

Like Season Nine, Sydney FC's Season Eleven was pretty rubbish overall, but this final game was a lot of fun.

A four–nil drubbing. It's always fun to beat Perth.

This was little Archie's second birthday, and his second Sydney FC match—his first had been a trip on the train to Olympic Park to watch Sydney play Newcastle.

Which, incidentally, had Ali Abbas come on as a late substitute—his first match after his return from injuries suffered in that Sydney derby a year before.

And he scored a goal pretty much straight away.

Amazing.

To be honest, Archie was more interested in the giant screen at the end of the pitch, up above The Cove.

And occasionally—when he wasn't wriggling, trying to draw on the seats with crayons, reading picture books or scoffing fish and chips—he would look up at the screen and yell out:

'BALL! BALL! BALL!'

Good work, son.

Good work.

All the goals are great.

David Carney's persistence in pouncing on a rebound.

Filip Holosko's solo run to score a goal from nothing.

But the third goal from Ali Abbas was just glorious—precision, focus, but—more importantly—hunger.

This sense of hunger has felt lacking all season—a will to win, to press forward, to stumble, but to recover and fight onward regardless.

It's been another scrappy season, and we don't make the finals again.

But right at the end of the season, with this sweeping victory there was something to cause genuine joy.

Something to justify continuing to be a Sydney FC fan.

Football, as I am far from the first to discover, is about *loyalty*, *hope* and *disappointment*.

Once again, we had lots of disappointment this season, but at the very last gasp, some hope.

From which loyalty endures.

I know my team is often shit.

I know that they don't *really* care about me, no matter what they say to the contrary.

I know that our players make bad decisions.

I know that our owners will have confusing priorities.

I know that our coach will make baffling choices.

I know that we will lose as often as we win.

I know that there will be many, many lean years.

I know that the referee will make a terrible decision and cost us the game.

I know that someone will have a brain snap and cost us the game.

I know that the team will get so so close and fall agonisingly short at the last minute.

But none of that matters.

Not really.

They're my team.

And I'll be in the stands again for the next home game, anxiously ready for kick-off.

Thank you and goodnight.

THE END

GTC RIVERSIDE NATIONAL THEATRE
GRIFFIN THEATRE COMPANY OF PARRAMATTA

NATIONAL THEATRE OF PARRAMATTA AND
GRIFFIN THEATRE COMPANY PRESENT

SMURF IN WANDERLAND
BY DAVID WILLIAMS

Director Lee Lewis
With David Williams
Set and Costume Designer Charles Davis
Lighting Designer Luiz Pampolha
Sound Designer and Composer James Brown
Dramaturg Kate Worsley
Creative Futures Participant Nick Atkins
Stage Manager Kirsty Walker
Production Manager Damion Holling

RIVERSIDE THEATRES
20 - 29 APRIL
SBW STABLES THEATRE
2 - 13 MAY

The development of *Smurf in Wanderland* was supported by the
NSW Government through Arts NSW, Griffin Theatre Company
through the 2015 Griffin Studio, Brand X as part of its 2014 Performing
Arts Residency Program, and the Rex Cramphorn Studio's
Artists-in-Residence Program, in Performance Studies at the
University of Sydney.

Partners

CITY OF PARRAMATTA   RIVERSIDE   CROWN RESORTS FOUNDATION   PACKER FAMILY FOUNDATION

Australian Government   Australia Council for the Arts   NSW GOVERNMENT | Arts NSW

This show began life as a joke.

I've been making various forms of 'reality' or 'non-fiction' theatre for the past fifteen years about a wide range of subjects, and I joked several times to friends that if I ever made a show about football, then I could claim my club membership as a tax deduction.

The more times I told this joke, the more surprised I was that people kept nodding seriously. "Yes", they would always say, "that'd be a really interesting show. I'd like to see that show."

Matters came to a head on the final day of the 2013 Australian Theatre Forum in Canberra. There was a panel of festival directors talking politely about their programming imperatives and blah blah blah, and then at the end there was a call for questions.

It was the last day. My brain/mouth filter had pretty much dissolved.

I raised my hand.

"Will any of your festivals be doing anything in conjunction with the Asian Football Cup, to be played in Australia in January 2015?"

Blank looks and silence ensued.

I felt like most people in the room were looking at me as if I'd grown a second head.

In the coffee break afterwards, Lee Lewis bounded up to me and said, "Great question. Are *you* doing anything?"

Put on the spot, I replied with my regular joke: "No, but I always thought that I *should* make a show about football, which would make my Sydney FC membership tax deductible."

"How would you make this show?" she asked.

I responded with the first idea that came into my head.

"Well, I suppose I could spend a season going to Western Sydney Wanderers' home games wearing Sydney FC colours, and talk to people."

She replied immediately. "I want to program that show."

It's taken a while, but four years later, here we are.

Smurf in Wanderland may have started as a joke, but it has proved to be a far more personal work than I ever imagined.

Over the past fifteen years, I've built a professional reputation around crafting theatre works from the words of other people – from public inquires, parliamentary proceedings, and interviews. I had genuinely believed that *Smurf in Wonderland* would be a work of a similar ilk.

But I found that the show only came alive when I placed myself in the narrative. And the result is the show you see tonight – a very personal account of football and Sydney.

My thanks to the great team that have so ably assisted me in realising this work – especially Kate, James and Lee who have been there from very early on, and have been amazingly supportive in shaping this strange little set of scribbles and ramblings into something more-or-less resembling a theatre show. Thanks to the National Theatre of Parramatta and Griffin Theatre Company for coming on board to produce and present *Smurf in Wanderland* – it is a great privilege to be a part of your 2017 seasons. Special thanks to my partner Suzie and our son Archie – in part for indulging my emerging football obsession, but mostly for going with me on this journey, knowing all the while that much of it would end up being material for a show.

And finally, this is a show about being a fan. In making this show, I've been inspired by the wonderful passion of the fans of both Sydney FC and the Western Sydney Wanderers.

A Sydney FC fan banner recently declared: OUR EXISTENCE DEFINES YOU.

A recent Wanderers banner declared: OUR BIRTH WAS YOUR DEATH.

I think it's fair to say that we've made each other stronger, and will continue to do so.

Bring on the next derby match, and Forza Sydney FC!

David Williams
Writer

I know David Williams as one of this country's greatest theatre philosophers. As fierce a practitioner as he is theoretician, when his gaze falls on a fault line in our society, his theatrical method of exposing it will always be subtle, rigorous, honest, unforgiving and inspiring.

This piece of reality theatre he has written is as deceptive as it is important. Coming to you in the disarming guise of a one man show, what may look like a simple love letter to the idea of 'fans' is actually a revealing analysis of modern cultural identity and a passionate artist's refusal to blithely accept governmental agenda and media laziness collaborating to denigrate the sport, the people and the city he loves.

It is work like this that tells me our artists will lead the way out of the quagmire of political idiocy in which we currently find ourselves. Smurf in Wanderland asserts that there is no division in Sydney that is not manipulated by insecure government living in fear of the short election cycle; that there is no division in Sydney that will not be exploited by the failing sensationalist media to bolster diminishing sales. It proves that our people are smarter than both institutions give them credit for. It is a funny, personal, moving act of political defiance.

Smurf in Wanderland is about football in Sydney. It is about passion. It is about how looking closely and understanding deeply can create a path towards a more hopeful future. It will not help you decide which team to follow in the A League.
But you've gotta have a team.

I am so proud to have a small part in bringing this play to the National Theatre of Parramatta and Griffin seasons.

Lee Lewis
Director

David Williams
Playwright and Performer

David Williams is a leading Australian theatre artist whose productions open spaces for public conversation about political and social issues. David was the Curator of ATF 2015: MAKING IT, and has worked for 20 years as a director, writer, producer, dramaturg, and performer with companies across Australia including Ilbijerri, Griffin, Queensland Theatre, Merrigong Theatre Company, Vitalstatistix, Belvoir, Branch Nebula, Sidetrack Performance Group, Sydney Theatre Company, Urban Theatre Projects and pvi collective.

He is a past winner of the Marten Bequest Traveling Scholarship for Acting, a graduate of the Australia Council's Emerging Leaders Development Program, a member of the 2015 Griffin Studio, and his theatre works have won Helpmann, Green Room and Drovers Awards. David was the founder and artistic leader of the performance group version 1.0, and co-created and produced all of the company's work from 1998 until parting ways with the company in 2012. These works included: *The Tender Age* (with ATYP), *The Disappearances Project, The Table of Knowledge* (with Merrigong Theatre Company), *The Bougainville Photoplay Project, THIS KIND OF RUCKUS, A Distressing Scenario, Deeply Offensive and Utterly Untrue, The Wages of Spin, CMI (A Certain Maritime Incident), From a Distance* and *The Second Last Supper*.

He holds a Doctor of Philosophy from the University of New South Wales, an Honours degree in Theatre from UWS (Nepean), and is currently an Honorary Associate at the Department of Performance Studies, University of Sydney, a committee member of SAMAG, and the Producer/Programmer at the Seymour Centre.

Under the banner DW Projects, David Williams creates theatre works of social relevance, aesthetic rigour and emotional impact from research, interviews, transcripts and public documents. Current and upcoming DW Projects include: *Quiet Faith* (national tour April-July 2018), *Smurf in Wanderland* (National Theatre of Parramatta & Griffin Theatre Company) and *Grace Under Pressure* (Seymour Centre & The Big Anxiety). *Smurf in Wanderland* is David's first work for National Theatre of Parramatta.

Lee Lewis

Director

Lee is the Artistic Director of Griffin Theatre Company and one of Australia's leading directors. For Griffin she has directed: *The Bleeding Tree* (for which Lee was awarded Best Director at the 2016 Helpmann Awards), *The Homosexuals, or 'Faggots', Eight Gigabytes of Hardcore Pornography, Masquerade* (co-directed with Sam Strong), *Gloria, Emerald City, A Rabbit for Kim Jong-il, The Serpent's Table* (co-directed with Darren Yap), *Replay, Silent Disco, The Bull, The Moon and the Coronet of Stars, The Call, A Hoax* and *The Nightwatchman*; for Griffin and Bell Shakespeare: *The Literati*; for Bell Shakespeare: *The School for Wives* and *Twelfth Night*; for Belvoir: *That Face, This Heaven, Half and Half, A Number, 7 Blowjobs* and *Ladybird*; for Melbourne Theatre Company (MTC): David Williamson's *Rupert*, which toured to Washington DC as part of the World Stages International Arts Festival and to Sydney's Theatre Royal in 2014; for STC: *Honour, Love-Lies-Bleeding* and *ZEBRA!*; for Darwin Festival: *Highway of Lost Hearts*; for the National Institute of Dramatic Art (NIDA): *Big Love, Shopping and Fucking, After Dinner* and *The Winter's Tale*; and for the Western Australian Academy of Performing Arts (WAAPA): *As You Like It*. This is Lee's first production with National Theatre of Parramatta.

Charles Davis

Set and Costume Designer

Charles is a Set and Costume Designer for theatre, opera, dance and film. Credits include: for Old Fitz: *The Whale*; for Queensland Conservatorium Theatre: *Hansel and Gretel*, (dir. Michael Gow); for Seymour Centre: *Unfinished Works*; for Sydney Chamber Opera/Sydney Festival: *Biographica, Oh Mensch!*; for Sydney Grammar: *The Grand Hotel*. Charles designed the set for the world premiere of Stephen Sewell's *Kandahar Gate* and set and costumes for Michael Gow's *Writing For Performance* (NIDA). His Assistant Designer credits include: for Belvoir: *The Great Fire, Twelfth Night*; for Carriageworks: *Lake Disappointment*; for Melbourne Theatre Company: *North By Northwest*, assisting Nick Schlieper and Simon Phillips in designing miniatures for the production. Charles studied architecture at Monash University and is a recent graduate of NIDA (Design). During his final year at NIDA, he was awarded the William Fletcher Foundation Award for emerging artists. Charles is now a lecturer and mentor for NIDA's undergraduate design program.

Luiz Pampolha

Lighting Designer

Luiz was the Lighting Designer for Griffin's *A Rabbit for Kim Jong-il, The Call, Concussion, Emerald City, Gloria, The Kid, The Nightwatchman, The Serpent's Table,* and *The Story Of The Miracles At Cookie's Table*. His other Lighting Designer credit include: for Australian Chamber Orchestra (ACO): *Kreutzer vs Kreutzer*; for Bell Shakespeare: *Twelfth Night*, for which Luiz was nominated for a Green Room Award; for Belvoir: *Antigone, Brothers Wreck, Don't Take Your Love To Town, This Heaven, Ruben Guthrie*; for Inscription in association with B Sharp: *Love*, for which Luiz was nominated for a Sydney Theatre Award; for Marguerite Pepper Productions: *Happy As Larry*; for Pinchgut Opera: *Castor et Pollux, The Chimney Sweep, Griselda*; for Sydney Chamber Opera: *The Cunning Little Vixen*; for Sydney Opera House: *The CODA Collective, danceTank, Emergence*; and for Sydney Theatre Company: *The 7 Stages of Grieving, Hip, Love-Lies-Bleeding*, for which Luiz was nominated for a Sydney Theatre Award, *Rabbit, The Removalists, Romeo & Juliet, Saturn's Return, Waiki*. Luiz is a graduate of NIDA, and a member of the Illuminating Engineering Society of Australia and New Zealand. This is Luiz's first production with National Theatre of Parramatta.

James Brown

Sound Designer and Composer

This is James' first production with National Theatre of Parramatta. He was the Sound and Video Designer for Griffin's *Tribunal*, co-produced by Powerhouse Youth Theatre. He has worked collaboratively with companies both locally and internationally to produce soundtracks for performance, film, animation and games. James has extensive experience working in collaborative, multi-artform processes and has formed ongoing artistic relationships, collaborating with artists and companies including: Bethesda, Victoria Hunt, Jane Campion, Australian Ballet, Sydney Dance Company, William Yang, George Khut, Matthew Day, Hans Van Den Broeck (SOIT), POST, and Urban Theatre Projects. He holds a Visual Arts degree from Sydney College of the Arts, and a Masters Degree in Acoustic Physics from Sydney University.

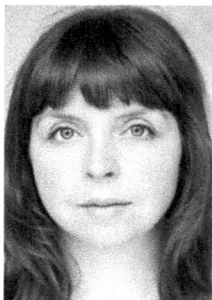

Kate Worsley

Dramaturg

Kate Worsley is an actor, theatremaker, voice-over and teaching artist. Kate was the first participant of National Theatre of Parramatta's Creative Futures program, where she worked on their inaugural show *Swallow*, directed by Kate Champion. She is a founding ensemble member of Clockfire Theatre Company where she co-devised *Lei Hideaway* (Best Theatre Show, Sydney Fringe 2012) and *The Grief Parlour* (Old 505 Theatre & TRUE WEST). As an actor she has toured extensively with Monkey Baa Theatre Company and also worked for Siren Theatre Co, Sydney Theatre Company, Darlinghurst Theatre Company and Brown's Mart, Darwin. She has performed in a number of award-winning short films including Y2GAY for which she was awarded Best Female Actor at Tropfest 2011. Kate has directed education and youth theatre projects for Riverside Theatres Education, ATYP and PYT including *The Letters Project, In This Fairfield: Romeo & Juliet In The West* (with David Williams) and *SUBURBIST*. She works as a teaching artist for Sydney Theatre Company, Bell Shakespeare and Joan Sutherland Performing Arts Centre and specialises in teaching English language learners.

Nick Atkins

Creative Futures Participant

Nick is a theatremaker and producer. He is currently Producer, Q Programs for The Joan and Board Member for PACT Centre for Emerging Artists. Nick has worked as Associate Producer and Co-Artistic Director of Crack Theatre Festival, and as a teaching artist for The Joan, Shopfront Contemporary Arts, Casula Powerhouse and ATYP. His directing credits include *Teacup in a Storm* and *Frankenstein*. Nick's play *Out of the Bars* won Gasworks Arts Park's 'Playtime' initiative in 2016. He wrote and performed *A Boy & A Bean*, which was awarded Best Performing Arts Event at Mardi Gras in 2014. Other productions include *Twinkle* (The Q, Seymour Centre), *Dance Hall Days*, directed by Katrina Douglas (The Q), and *Unsex Me*, which was part of Riverside's 'True West Theatre' program.

Kirsty Walker

Stage Manager

Kirsty was Stage Manager for National Theatre of Parramatta's *The Cartographer's Curse*. This is her first production with Griffin. Her credits as Stage Manager include: for Don't Look Away: *Inner Voices, The Legend of King O'Malley*, for which she was also the FOH Mixer; for the Glynn Nicholas Group: *Song Contest: The Almost Eurovision Experience*. Kirsty's credits as Assistant Stage Manager include: for Belvoir: *Kill the Messenger*; for Melbourne Opera: *The Abduction from the Seraglio, Anna Bolena, Tannhäuser*. She was the FOH Mixer in the 2015 Edinburgh Festival Fringe. Kirsty is a NIDA graduate (Production).

Damion Holling

Production Manager

Damion is a graduate of the Liverpool Institute of Performing Arts (LIPA) 2003. Prior to moving to Australia in 2008, he worked extensively in the UK and Europe, including working in London's West End and for various regional venues. In Australia, Damion has worked as Production Manager with Kim Carpenters' Theatre of Image, Sydney Chamber Opera, Michael Sieders Presents, Legs on the Wall, and for numerous national and international tours, major festivals and events. Since 2009, Damion has been the Site and Construction Manager for Sydney Festival's Domain Concert site. Damion has worked on National Theatre of Parramatta's past three productions.

ABOUT NATIONAL THEATRE OF PARRAMATTA

Riverside's Resident Company

Having burst onto the Australian theatre scene in 2016, with four acclaimed new theatre works, National Theatre of Parramatta (NTofP) continues in 2017 with four world premieres, exciting commissions and creative developments which we look forward to sharing with you in the future.

National Theatre of Parramatta aspires to create bold, contemporary works that draw their inspiration from the rich diversity of Western Sydney and beyond, adding to our cultural landscape is a company that reflects the nation on stage.

Integral to our Company is the development of Western Sydney's professional and emerging artists. We aim to build generations of exciting and challenging theatre-makers, capable of making work of the highest quality, for a range of audiences, with and for National Theatre of Parramatta and the wider theatre sector.

In 2016 NTofP launched a range of behind the scenes programs that build capacity for the performing arts in New South Wales with playwriting programs, mentorships, professional and creative development programs, industry talks, networking opportunities, engagement for young people and audience outreach programs.

National Theatre of Parramatta
PO Box 3636,
Parramatta NSW 2124

+61 2 8839 3385
admin@nationaltheatreofparramatta.com.au
nationaltheatreofparramatta.com.au

Facebook.com/nationaltheatreofparramatta
Twitter @NTofP
Instagram @ntofp

RIVERSIDE | NATIONAL THEATRE OF PARRAMATTA

Partners

RIVERSIDE

CITY OF PARRAMATTA

NSW GOVERNMENT | Arts NSW

CROWN RESORTS FOUNDATION

PACKER FAMILY FOUNDATION

NATIONAL THEATRE OF PARRAMATTA DIRECTORATE & STAFF

Directorate
Annette Shun Wah
S. Shakthidharan
Wayne Harrison AM

Executive Producer
Joanne Kee

Company Coordinator
Clare Spillman

Marketing Coordinator
Claire Cornu

Administrator
Cassandra Bayley

Traineeship
Stefanie Dellzeit

Riverside Theatres

Director
Robert Love

Business Manager
Pamela Thornton

Operations Manager
Linda Taylor

Marketing and Communications Manager
Jonathan Llewellyn

SUPPORT
NATIONAL THEATRE
OF PARRAMATTA

We believe in developing work that celebrates the richness of our society, and its creative talent, and in the importance of providing opportunities for artists, writers and directors to develop their skills.

Whether you are an individual wishing to become a patron or make a donation, or a company seeking partnership opportunities, your support is invaluable to our continuing efforts to deliver exceptional work to the widest possible audience.

Every donation is valuable. All donations of $2 or more are tax-deductible. Donations can be made through Parramatta Cultural Trust.

For more information visit our website or contact Executive Producer, Joanne Kee on 02 8839 3385 or email jkee@nationaltheatreofparramatta.com.au.

THE INCREDIBLE HERE AND NOW

13–22 JULY 2017

Based on the award-winning novel by Felicity Castagna
Directed by Jeneffa Soldatic and Wayne Harrison
Adapted by Felicity Castagna

*Charcoal chicken, a white Pontiac Trans Am, the council pool. Michael
is living in the shadow of his older brother Dom. The biggest guy in the
school. Best car in the west.*

RIVERSIDE | NATIONAL THEATRE OF PARRAMATTA

THE RED TREE

19–28 OCTOBER 2017

Based on the book by Shaun Tan
Directed by Neil Gooding
Adapted by Hilary Bell
Music by Greta Gertler Gold
Designed by James Brown

The Red Tree explores the expressive possibilities of shared imagination in a new music theatre production.

NATIONAL THEATRE OF PARRAMATTA
RIVERSIDE

ABOUT DW PROJECTS

DW Projects represents the artistic output of theatre maker David Williams and collaborators – works of social relevance, aesthetic rigour and emotional impact.

Based around research, interviews, transcripts and public documents, DW Projects creates truly unique performances that open spaces for public conversation around matters of civic and political importance. Surprising, engaging, and elegantly constructed, the theatre of DW Projects explores contemporary social life in all its complexity, messiness, beauty and strangeness.

Since 2013, DW Projects has been developing a suite of theatre works that explore ideas of belief and belonging. *Quiet Faith,* co-commissioned by Vitalstatistix and HotHouse Theatre, explores the complex entanglements of religious faith and civic engagement. Quiet Faith premiered in 2014, and will tour nationally in 2018. *Smurf in Wanderland,* presented by National Theatre of Parramatta and Griffin Theatre Company, is a personal exploration of football fandom and geographic belonging in Sydney. *Really Big Democracy,* will investigate the complex experiences and perspectives of citizens of 'free' and 'democratic' nations. This is a collaboration with Budapest-based political theatre company PanoDrama, and commenced research and development in November 2015.

DW Projects' new suite of works (2017-2020) will explore work and life, investigating the complex institutional and interpersonal relationships that shape us. Future works include:

Grace Under Pressure

By David Williams and Paul Dwyer in collaboration
with the Sydney Arts and Health Collective

Co-commissioned by Seymour Centre and
The Big Anxiety Festival of Interactive Arts

World premiere October 2017

Medicine and nursing are often referred to as 'caring' professions, yet there is ample evidence of the damage that health and medical practitioners do to one another. Bullying, harassment and 'teaching by humiliation' are a common experience in hospitals, particularly for students and interns. Rates of clinical depression and anxiety, suicidal ideation and suicidal behaviour among this population are twice the national average (Beyond Blue, National Mental Health Survey of Doctors and Medical Students, 2013). Developed from interviews with interns, medical and nursing students, as well as senior allied health professionals and representatives from the specialist colleges, *Grace Under Pressure* examines the workplace and training cultures that are making young health professionals sick – and which put patient lives at risk.

Only Players

In development 2017

A verbatim theatre project built from interviews with high school English teachers in NSW schools about their experience of teaching Shakespeare. The age and experience ranges of these teachers will be diverse – some retired, some newly graduated, some from privileged 'elite' schools, others from struggling outer-urban schools, and others from small rural schools. *Only Players* will explore how education has changed over the past decades with declining state government investment and the increasing embrace of managerialism within the schools' system. By turns joyful, poignant and comedic, *Only Players* will provide a unique opportunity to reflect upon the future of the humanities in the contemporary Australian education system.

Internal Management Change

In development 2018

A conversation-based verbatim project that will explore the human impacts of small and large redundancies driven by drastic changes in industries and labour markets. What happens to your identity and sense of self-worth when you are informed that you have to re-apply for your job? Or told that your employer no longer requires your services? What are the lived experience of those jettisoned by restructures and 'efficiency dividends'? How do we rebuild? Should we re-skill, re-train, or retire? And what will we all do when the robots finally take our jobs?

ABOUT GRIFFIN

"If you've ever sat in the theatre and thought, 'those actors are just too damn far away', then Griffin is for you." – Concrete Playground

Located in the heart of Kings Cross – in the historic SBW Stables Theatre – Griffin has been dedicated to bringing the best Australian stories to the stage for the better part of four decades.

We're passionate about theatre that's written by Australians, about Australians, for Australians to enjoy. Iconic plays such as *The Boys, Holding the Man* and *The Heartbreak Kid* all had their world premieres at Griffin. And many of our nation's most celebrated artists started their professional careers with us – Cate Blanchett, David Wenham, Michael Gow and Louis Nowra to name a few.

Homegrown inspiration. By you, for you.

GRIFFIN THEATRE COMPANY
13 CRAIGEND ST
KINGS CROSS NSW 2011

02 9332 1052
INFO@GRIFFINTHEATRE.COM.AU
GRIFFINTHEATRE.COM.AU

SBW STABLES THEATRE
10 NIMROD ST
KINGS CROSS NSW 2011

BOOKINGS
GRIFFINTHEATRE.COM.AU
02 9361 3817

GTC
GRIFFIN
THEATRE
COMPANY

Australian Government
Australia Council for the Arts

NSW GOVERNMENT | Arts NSW

Griffin acknowledges the generosity of the Seaborn, Broughton & Walford Foundation in allowing it the use of the SBW Stables Theatre rent free, less outgoings, since 1986.

STAFF

Artistic Director & CEO
Lee Lewis

General Manager
Karen Rodgers

**Associate Producer -
Development**
Will Harvey

**Associate Producer -
Marketing**
Estelle Conley

Associate Producer
Nicole La Bianca

Publicist
Dino Dimitriadis

Communications Associate
Aurora Scott

**Marketing & Development
Coordinator**
Lucy McNabb

**Program and
Administration
Coordinator**
Madeleine Parker

**Strategic Insights
Consultant**
Peter O'Connell

Production Manager
Kirby Brierty

Financial Consultant
Tracey Whitby

Finance Manager
Kylie Richards

Customer Relations Manager
Elliott Wilshier

Front of House Manager
Damien Storer

Front of House
Maria Dimopulos, Alex
Herlihy, Renee Heys, Julian
Larnach, Jade da Silva,
Linda Popic

Studio Artist
Phil Spencer

Web Developer
Holly

Digital Consultant
Adrian Wiggins

Brand and Graphic Design
Re

Cover Photography
Brett Boardman

OUR
DONORS

Income from Griffin activities covers less than 40% of our operating costs – leaving an ever increasing gap for us to fill through government funding, sponsorship and the generosity of our individual supporters. Your support helps us bridge the gap and keep ticket prices affordable and our work at its best. To make a donation and a difference, contact Griffin on 9332 1052 or donate online at griffintheatre.com.au

OUR DONORS

Studio Program
Gil Appleton
James Emmett & Peter Wilson
Limb Family Foundation
Peter Graves
Sophie McCarthy & Antony Green
Ken & Lilian Horler
Rhonda McIver
Geoff & Wendy Simpson
Danielle Smith

PRODUCTION DONORS

THE HOMOSEXUALS OR 'FAGGOTS' 2017

Presenting Partner
Rebel Penfold-Russell

Production Patrons
Anonymous
Andrew Bell & Joanna Bird
Robert Dick & Erin Shiel
Richard McHugh & Kate Morgan
Bruce Meagher & Greg Waters
Penelope Wass
Richard Weinstein & Richard Benedict

Production Partners
Gil Appleton
Rodney Cambridge
Michael Hobbs
Tony Jones
Steve Riethoff
Diana Simmonds

SEASON DONORS

Commission $12,500+
Darin Cooper Foundation
Anthony & Suzanne Maple-Brown

Main Stage Donor $5,000 - $10,000
Peter Graves
Helen & Abraham James
Jon King
Don & Leslie Parsonage
Lee Lewis & Brett Boardman
Sue Procter
The Robertson Family Foundation
Merilyn Sleigh & Raoul de Ferranti

Final Draft $2,000-$4,999
Gae Anderson
Stewart Baxter
Ellen Borda
Alex Byrne & Sue Hearn
Richard Cottrell
Mark Coulter
Bryony & Tim Cox
Tina & Maurice Green
Libby Higgin
Sophie McCarthy & Antony Green
Bruce Meagher & Greg Waters
David Nguyen
Peter & Dianne O'Connell
Pip Rath & Wayne Lonergan
Anthony Paull
Chris Reed
Westpac
Adrian Wiggins & Siobhan Toohill
Carole & David Yuile

Workshop Donor $1,000-$1,999
Anonymous (3)
Antoinette Albert
Melissa Ball
Baly Douglass Foundation
Karen Bedford
Amanda Bishop
Jane Bridge
Corinne Campbell & Bryan Everts

Ange Cecco & Melanie Bienemann
Terence Clarke
Russ & Rae Cottle
Michael Diamond
Tim Duggan
Ros & Paul Epsie
John & Libby Fairfax
Jennifer Giles
Judge Joe Harman
James Hartwright & Kerrin D'Arcy
John Head
Angela Herscovitch
Michael Hobbs
Peter Ingle
Margaret Johnston
Jennifer Ledgar & Bob Lim
Kiong Lee & Richard Funston
Richard & Elizabeth Longes
Elaine & Bill McLaughlin
Ruth Melville
Dr Wendy Michaels
Stephen Mills
Tommy Murphy
Jo Nolan
Patricia Novikoff
Martin Portus
Crispin Rice
Rebecca Rocheford Davies
Natalie Shea
Will Sheehan
Amanda and Michael Solomon
Ross Steele
Augusta Supple
Victoria Taylor
Stuart Thomas
Mike Thompson
Gayle Tollifson
Anna Volska
Judy & Sam Weiss
Paul & Jennifer Winch
Penny Young & Ian Neuss

OUR
DONORS

Reading Donor $500-$999
Anonymous (4)
Jes Andersen
Wendy Ashton
Robyn Ayres
Michael Barnes
Penny Beran
Edwina Birch
Michael & Colleen
Chesterman
Sally Crawford
Carol Dettmann
Fiona Dewar
Louise Diamond
Max Dingle
Vicki Ditcham
Wendy Elder
Erica Gray
Sheba Greenberg
Anthony Gregg
Janet Grant
Jennifer Hagan
Stephanie & Andrew
Harrison
Jacqueline Hayes
Tim & Virginia Herlihy
Mark Hopkinson
Sylvia Hrovatin
Susan Hyde
C John Keightley
Ian & Elizabeth MacDonald
Rob Macfarlan & Nicole
Abadee
Carina Martin
Christopher McCabe
John McCallum
Stuart McLean
Dr Steve McNamara
Neville Mitchell
Catriona Morgan-Hunn
Steve & Belinda Rankine
Alex Oonagh Redmond
Roslyn Renwick
Annabel Ritchie

Karen Rodgers & Bill
Harris
Julianne Schultz
Nicola Scott
Diana Simmonds
Jann Skinner
Eric Dole & Mary Stollery
Adam Suckling
Catherine Sullivan &
Alexandra Bowen
Sue Thomson
Jennifer Watson
Simone Whetton

**Griffin Theatre Company
would also like to
gratefully acknowledge
all our supporters who
have contributed up
to $500: far too many
to mention in this
small program!**

Current as of
24 February, 2017

GRIFFIN SPONSORS

Griffin would like to thank the following:

Government Supporters

Australian Government | Australia Council for the Arts

CREATIVE CITY SYDNEY

NSW GOVERNMENT | Arts NSW

Patron

2017 Season Sponsor

Production Partner

Production Sponsors

GIRGENSOHN FOUNDATION

nabprivate / nab

 FOXTEL arts

Foundations and Trusts

 MALCOLM ROBERTSON FOUNDATION

COPYRIGHT AGENCY CULTURAL FUND

ROBERTSON FOUNDATION

GIRGENSOHN FOUNDATION

Company Lawyers

Associate Sponsors

MAR/QUE

Brett Boardman Photography

ive

Company Sponsors

TimeOut

THE UNIVERSITY OF SYDNEY PERFORMANCE STUDIES

Tatler SYDNEY

bourke street bakery

Rosenfeld, Kant & Co. Business & Financial Solutions

MOPPITY

CURRENCY PRESS

Coopers

PROUDLY EST. 2013 FOUR PILLARS SMALL AUSTRALIAN DISTILLERY

 DARLINGHURST

Qbt CONSULTING

THE SATURDAY PAPER

DESIGNKINGCOMPANY

Griffin Theatre Company is assisted by the Australian Government through the Australia Council, its arts funding and advisory body; and the NSW Government through Arts NSW.

CURRENCY PLAYS

THE BLEEDING TREE
Angus Cerini

In a dirt-dry town in rural Australia, a shot shatters the still night. A mother and her daughters have just welcomed home the man of the house - with a crack in the shins and a bullet in the neck. The only issue now is disposing of the body. Triggered into thrilling motion by an act of revenge, The Bleeding Tree is rude, rhythmical and irreverently funny. Imagine a murder ballad blown up for the stage, set against a deceptively deadly Aussie backdrop, with three fierce females fighting back. Winner of: the Griffin Award (2014), a Sydney Theatre Award for Best New Australian Work (2015), an AWGIE Award (2016), a Helpmann Award: Best Play (2016), and the NSW Premier's Literary Award: Playwriting (2016).

978-1-76062-046-2, also available as an ebook

MICHAEL SWORDFISH
Lachlan Philpott

What would happen if someone you knew disappeared? How would you react? How would your school react? An assembly called, a footy game postponed, a class interrupted. But who is Michael Swordfish? And who knows where he's gone? For two years award-winning playwright Lachlan Philpott collaborated with students from Newington College, Sydney, to bring their voices and worlds to life. Michael Swordfish is the exciting product of this collaboration: a play that traverses the tumultuous landscape of the teenage experience with a sober truth and darkly comic voice.

978-1-76062-083-7, also available as an ebook

MARK COLVIN'S KIDNEY
Tommy Murphy

A premiere Australian play based on actual events, showing just how startling real-life can be. Mary-Ellen Field is a successful Australian business consultant in London– until she's accused of betraying the secrets of her supermodel client to the press. Her life comes crashing down: her job, her health and her standing in society collapse. When it emerges that her client's phone had been hacked by reporters, Mary Ellen sets out to defiantly restore her reputation. But along the way, her ideas of redemption change–she's been interviewed by a journalist on the other side of the world, and his story puts everything into a new perspective.

978-1-76062-001-1, also available as an ebook

www.currency.com.au

Visit Currency Press' website now to:

- Buy your books online
- Browse through our full list of titles, from plays to screenplays, books on theatre, film and music, and more
- Choose a play for your school or amateur performance group by cast size and gender
- Obtain information about performance rights
- Find out about theatre productions and other performing arts news across Australia
- For students, read our study guides
- For teachers, access syllabus and other relevant information
- Sign up for our email newsletter

The performing arts publisher